ASTROLOGY OF SUCCESS

*A guide to illuminate your
inborn gifts for achieving career
success and life fulfillment*

JAN SPILLER

The opinions expressed in this manuscript are solely the opinions of the author and do not represent the opinions or thoughts of the publisher. The author has represented and warranted full ownership and/or legal right to publish all the materials in this book.

The Astrology of Success
A Guide to Illuminate Your Inborn Gifts for Achieving Career Success and Life Fulfillment
All Rights Reserved
Copyright © 2014 Jan Spiller
V8.0 R1.1

Cover Photo © 2014 JupiterImages Corporation. All rights reserved - used with permission.

Astrological glyphs by Kerry Tinney

This book may not be reproduced, transmitted, or stored in whole or in part by any means, including graphic, electronic, or mechanical without the express written consent of the publisher except in the case of brief quotations embodied in critical articles and reviews.

Outskirts Press, Inc.
http://www.outskirtspress.com

ISBN 978-1-4327-9198-8

Outskirts Press and the "OP" logo are trademarks belonging to Outskirts Press, Inc.

PRINTED IN THE UNITED STATES OF AMERICA

About The Author

JAN SPILLER is known throughout the world as a trusted and perceptive leader in astrology. She is an innovator in using astrology as a definitive tool that links her readers to their individual spiritual path. Thus her books both illuminate her readers' way and empower them to manifest their dreams. Her books are based on her unique personal approach to the inner working of the human psyche and its connection with spiritual empowerment.

She has websites both in America and Japan, teaches regularly at New Age and astrology conferences, and is a highly sought after radio and television guest.

Her books, Cosmic Love, Astrology for the Soul, New Moon Astrology, and Spiritual Astrology are published internationally, and are currently available in 18 languages. She is currently working on another book soon to be released with an in-depth look at the Sun Signs, as well as a book on the North Node Houses. Jan lives in New York City; Del Mar, California; and Charleston, South Carolina.

Also By Jan Spiller

Cosmic Love

New Moon Astrology

Astrology for the Soul

Spiritual Astrology

https://www.janspiller.com/books.php

Contents

Preface 1

Introduction 3

The Basic Formula 6

How To Use This Book 16

Chapter 1: Key To Success
   Your Midheaven 23
Aries 23
Taurus 27
Gemini 31
Cancer 35
Leo 39
Virgo 42
Libra 46
Scorpio 50
Sagittarius 53
Capricorn 57
Aquarius 61
Pisces 65

Chapter 2: Resources for Pursuing Goals
   The House Containing Your 10th House Ruler 69

1st House 69
2nd House 70
3rd House 72
4th House 73
5th House 74
6th House 75
7th House 76
8th House 77
9th House 79
10th House 80
11th House 81
12th House 82

Chapter 3: Special Talents
Planets Located in 10th House 84
Sun 84
Moon 86
Mercury 89
Venus 91
Mars 93
Jupiter 96
Saturn 98
Uranus 101
Neptune 104
Plute 107
North Node in the 10the House 109
South Node in the 10th Houe 111
Two or more Planets in the 10th House 112
No Planets in the 10th House 113

Chapter 4: Additional Assets for Success ....
Houses Ruled by 10th House Planets 115

1st House 115
2nd House 116
3rd House 117
4th House 117
5th House 118
6th House 118
7th House 119
8th House 120
9th House 120
10th House 121
11th House 121
12th House 122

Chapter 5: Qualities that Can Help Further Your Career
            Your Saturn Sign 123

Conclusion 129

Preface

The astrology chart is where the "karma" (the Soul's record of past lives) and the "dharma" (the path the Soul has chosen to walk this lifetime) of each individual are revealed. These will play out according to the evolutionary level and intention of the Soul that chose to incarnate in that frequency. Your chart is like a special mirror that reflects your unique, natural internal wiring, just as a regular mirror reflects your "external presentation" - your physical body.

This is the element of "fate" that many people experience operating in their lives, and it can be seen in the astrology chart. But even though you cannot change your internal wiring any more than you can change the height or bone structure of your physical body, you *can* choose how to adapt and use what has been given to you to your advantage. When you use astrology to become aware of your internal wiring, you can consciously choose how you want to work with it.

By accepting and cooperating with this "blueprint", you have the power to create your own destiny and lead a happy and fulfilling life. It is only when you resist "what is" that you become dissatisfied, frustrated, and rail against life. Conscious awareness and acceptance of your unique path of growth - and that of others - is the key to experiencing inner freedom and peacefulness.

2   The Astrology of Success

As each person reads the material in this book, only *they* will know which of the gifts mentioned triggers a "chord" in them and points to a successful career. Even as children, we all have had insights showing us a career path to follow that we felt excited about. Intuitively you already know the answer, and this material is presented to activate and validate your innate gifts for successfully realizing your goals.

Jan Spiller

Introduction

This book is intended as a guide in actualizing that part of you that seeks a meaningful role in the world. The 10th House spotlights the inborn talents you feel compelled to express, the activities that bring you happiness, and what you are best at. It also shows the qualities you are meant to develop, experience and share in this lifetime. These are the gifts and tools that you have for establishing a tangible success in any area of life.

Once you are consciously aware of where your power to manifest lies, you can initiate lines of action that are in alignment with your internal wiring. This is the path most likely to lead to success, because it is when you are expressing these natural talents that others are most likely to go along with your plans.

I hope as you read through these pages you experience a lot of "aha" moments. These insights can connect the talents listed with what you've always felt drawn to do. A gift may be used in many different ways. For example, the gift of being able to create art and beauty and harmony can be applied to a wide variety of professions: interior decorator, painter, stylist, diplomat, etc. As you read the descriptions given, you will instinctively know which profession is right for you.

By expressing your 10th House talents in the ways described in this book, you will naturally choose work you are good at - and thus be successful. This is the path that leads to financial prosperity, status, career satisfaction, and a sense of fulfillment. On a personal level, when you express your 10th House gifts you create successful outcomes in terms of relationships and in achieving other personal goals that are important to you.

As an example, if one's 10th House is ruled by Gemini, the person will experience professional success by choosing a career path in a Gemini-related field such as writing, teaching, sales, etc. They will reach personal goals by approaching each situation from a strictly logical point of view and when they remember to take the thinking of others into account. They can experience success in personal relationships by going out of their way to keep the lines of communication open and seeking to understand how the other person thinks, their point of view, and what interests them.

For 10th House Gemini people, when they "get curious" they win. For them, focusing on open communication is the key to being successful in love, partnership, work, money, family, etc.

Your 10th House also has to do with your purpose on earth, why you are here in the first place. It is the highest point in the chart, and reveals – on a soul level – talents you are meant to share and what you have promised to contribute to society in this lifetime. By fulfilling this promise, your character is strengthened and the ability to lead a healthy and balanced life is activated.

I would be remiss not to mention that in astrology, attaining material success has to do not only with status, career, and goal achievement as shown by the 10th House, but also with the handling and accumulation of money, which is shown by the 2nd House in the natal chart. The 6th House shows the kind of day-to-day work that will be satisfying for the individual, also a part of true success.

Thus the material success houses are Houses 10, 2, and 6. This book covers House 10. The second book in the wealth series, which will cover the 2nd and 6th Houses, is in the process of being written. If you enter your email address on the mailing list at janspiller.com you will be notified when the second book is released.

The Basic Formula

There is a basic astrological formula for understanding an individual's karma - how they are "wired" - in all areas of life: 1) Look at the house that rules the area of interest (money, love, health, career, etc); 2) identify the planet ruling that house; 3) look at the house in which this planetary ruler resides, other planets located in the house of interest (if any), and the houses ruled by each of those planets.

In this book I have applied this basic formula to the 10th House - the house of worldly success. The same formula can be applied to understanding how you are designed in all other areas of life.

The following are brief descriptions of the areas ruled by the houses. There are many more "keywords" for each house. A good book for finding keywords is Alan Oken's *Complete Astrology*.

1st House – body and personality

2nd House – money, personal values, possessions

3rd House – communication, social ease, siblings, learning/teaching, writing

4th House – home, family, frame of reference

5th House – romance, personal love, creativity, children, pleasure

6th House – work, health, personal organization, job, projects, routines, pets

7th House – partnership, marriage, team efforts

8th House – joint bonded ventures, partnerships: sexual or financial, contracts

9th House – the law, philosophy, travel, peace of mind

10th House – success, profession, public status, goal achievement

11th House – friends, humanitarian causes, hopes and dreams, seeing the future

12th House – your private vision, mystical pursuits, self-sabotaging patterns, psychic insights

EXAMPLE CHARTS

These charts and partial 10th House interpretations are included to show you some of the ways astrological information can play out in a person's life.

Steve Jobs, born: February 24, 1955, 7:15 pm, San Francisco, CA

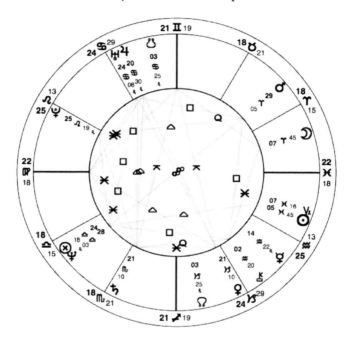

Midheaven - Gemini
House containing the 10th House Ruler - House 5
Planet(s) located in the 10th House - South Node, Jupiter, Uranus
Houses Ruled by 10th House Planet(s) - 4th and 6th

With the South Node in his 10th House, when Jobs' focus was on power and control over his own company - Apple - he was fired in 1985. When he pulled back and re-focused on his foundation (shown by his North Node in House 4) - his passion for loving the *process* of what he did - his success was huge and changed the world. With the ruler of House 10 in House 5, his specialty was creating products that were entertaining for people. It is interesting that his Uranus is technically in the 10th House, but close to the 11th. He pulled on 11th House gifts (invention, connecting with the future) in furthering his business.

Oprah Winfrey, January 29, 1954, 4:30 am, Kosciusko, Mississippi

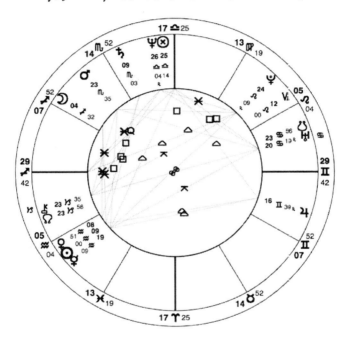

Midheaven - Libra
House containing the 10th House Ruler - House 2
Planet(s) located in the 10th House - Neptune and Saturn
Houses Ruled by 10th House Planet(s) - House 3 and House 1

The ruler of her Midheaven (Libra) is in her 2nd House, so her career was the gateway through which she expressed her personal values. Neptune in the 10th House shows that she has a sense of mission and that part of her success will be in promoting spiritual or artistic values. With Libra ruling her Midheaven, the strong one-to-one connections she creates when interviewing guests was the key to her attaining public success.

Muhammad Ali, born: January 17, 1942, 6:35 pm, Louisville, Kentucky

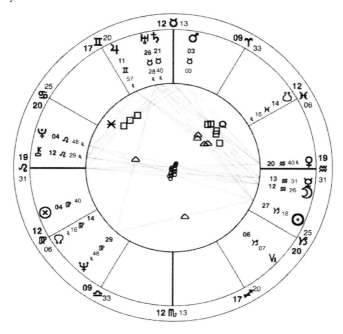

Midheaven - Taurus
House containing the 10th House Ruler - House 7
Planet(s) located in the 10th House - Saturn, Uranus, and Jupiter
Houses Ruled by 10th House Planet(s) - House 6, House 7, and House 5

With so many planets in his 10th House, his drive for career achievement and success was the main focus of his life. Having Sun and Moon in the 6th House makes him willing to do the hard work necessary. His practice of verbalizing his words of victory to gain an edge over his opponent is shown by his nodal axis in houses 2 and 8: it made him stronger and increased his self-worth when he was actively involved in merging the other person's psychology with his own ideas of how things would progress.

ELEMENTS

The elements are important in considering the natural temperamental affinity of the individual. Does the native have a disposition that is primarily emotional (water signs), intellectual (air signs), practical (earth signs), or creatively intense (fire signs)? For the experienced astrologer, all these factors are an influence in fine-tuning the information received from the basic formula outlined in The Astrology of Success.

ASPECTS

For a deeper understanding of the way an individual is internally wired, there is additional information an astrologer can access by looking at the "Aspects" between the planets. The element of "fate" that is involved in creating success in any area of life is largely determined by the Planetary Aspects involved. For example, if the planet that rules the house of interest is in harmony with another planet located in that house (a trine or sextile aspect), there will be easy good fortune in that area of the person's life. This is because internally they will not feel any conflict in satisfying the urges represented by both of these planets.

For example, if the planet ruling the 7th House (marriage) is in an harmonious aspect (trine or sextile) to a planet located in the 10th House (career), the individual will feel there is no problem between having a happy marriage or partnership and a successful career. In fact, they will have good luck in creating both, and these areas of their life will work together harmoniously (see Oprah Winfrey's chart).

Conversely, if the ruler of one house is in difficult aspect (a square or opposition) to a planet in that house - or the rulers of each house are in a difficult aspect with each other - the person will experience an internal tug of war and feel that they can't have both simultaneously.

For example, if the native has a square between a planet in the 7th House (marriage) and one in the 10th (career) it is not their fate to "fall into" both a happy marriage and a successful career working together harmoniously. Something within drives them to feel that they have to "choose" one thing or the other. Even if they do find themselves in a relationship that will support their career, subconsciously they will do something to either remove the relationship or neglect their career. For whatever reason, it may simply not be their destiny to experience both simultaneously in this lifetime (see the chart of Muhammad Ali).

As another example, I have a client who has the ruler of her 7th House (marriage) in her 1st House (autonomy) - opposing a planet in her 7th House. This creates internal conflict between her need for independence and her urge to partner in a marriage. She tends to lose herself in marriage, and then feels she has to leave the relationship in order to reclaim her independence. She is not "wired" to be able to see how she can be in a marriage and still maintain her independence.

In this particular case the matter is compounded by the fact that both planets are square to a planet in the 10th House (career). This creates internal conflict between the areas of marriage, independence, and career. She doesn't see how any of these three areas of life can work together smoothly because she isn't designed that way.

However, these conflicting forces do give her a strong focus and sense of excitement. Because of the stressful aspects, all three areas of her life are highly energized. She is constantly dealing with these issues - career vs. autonomy vs. partnership - with conscious attention, vigilance and deep understanding, trying to balance her attraction to each because they don't work smoothly together.

The practical question is how does she want to use that energy?

Needless to say, this has been a "learning and growing" lifetime for her! She has a successful, established career (10th House) that allows her autonomy (a 1st House need), and has been in and out of several marriages and partnerships (7th House). As of this writing, she seems quite happy with her life, which has had many chapters. What works for her at her current stage of life is different than how she chose to resolve this inner conflict in earlier years.

With harmonious aspects, we're naturally lucky and thus don't pay much attention to those areas of life - "If it ain't broke, don't fix it." What we focus on are the things that aren't working. Our choice is to consciously work to understand them more deeply, or complain and feel miserable. As you can see, understanding the ASPECTS between the planets can add richness and insights to the basic formula presented in this book.

For further information on aspects, go to janspiller.com and click on the astrology 101 section.

DEFINITION OF ASTROLOGICAL TERMS

Aspects show the energetic RELATIONSHIPS between the planetary urges and the houses those planets are associated with.

A circle has 360 degrees. Imagine that the planets are located in different positions around a wheel close to the outside edge. Each planet shoots a line of energy straight toward the center of the circle, and the way the energy connects between the planets is the way the wiring connects within ourselves.

Aspect of Conjunction is 0 degrees of separation between two planets, meaning that the two planets operate together. For example, if Venus conjoins Pluto, the urge to love and be loved (Venus) is linked with the desire for transformation and empowerment (Pluto). This person will attract love relationships that involve power struggles and necessitate personal growth and transformation through the arena of love.

Aspect of Square is 90 degrees of separation between two planets. The square shows an internal conflict. For example, if Mars is square Venus the person feels an internal conflict between love (Venus) and sex (Mars). The native often feels that they can't have both a satisfying sexual relationship and a happy love relationship with the same person. This experience of inner conflict often results in outer adjustment in the areas of life where the square exists.

Aspect of Opposition is 180 degrees of separation between two planets. The urges represented by the two planets involved are in conflict with each other, and conflict is experienced between those areas of life ruled by the houses involved. For example, if Mercury opposes the Moon, what the person thinks logically (Mercury) is in opposition with what they feel and need emotionally (Moon). It is relationships with others that stimulate the oppositions in the chart. Thus the person experiences outer struggle with others to have the needs of both planets satisfied. The opposition is like a teeter-totter, with the native either on one side or the other in terms of experiencing fulfillment of the two urges. The resolution is in consciously allotting time to each urge separately.

Aspect of Trine is 120 degrees of separation between two planets. This is an aspect of harmony and "good luck." Internally, the urges of both planets are naturally working together in a harmonious way. As a result of that internal harmony, spontaneous "good luck" is created in the external world. The person seems to "fall into" fortunate circumstances in the areas of life containing the Trine without much effort.

Aspect of Sextile is 60 degrees of separation between two planets. This aspect shows an area of natural inner comfort that, combined with applied effort, can result in good luck and material success in the outer world. The person seems to have the ability to combine their natural talents and use them to achieve success in the areas of life containing the sextile and ruled by the sextiling planets.

Elements: As used in astrology, the term "elements" refers to fire, earth, air and water. Each sign of the Zodiac falls into one of these four elements (Leo is a fire sign, Pisces is a water sign, etc.). The element in which each planet occurs describes the temperament and disposition of the individual.

Karma: Cause and effect; the results we experience from actions we have taken. In terms of Past Lives, Karma also has to do with the residue of unresolved issues prior to this lifetime that has determined the destiny or fate of the individual as seen in the natal chart.

Midheaven: The Midheaven and the Ascendant (Rising Sun) are mathematically calculated points on the astrology chart. The Ascendant is where the Sun passes the horizon; the Midheaven is where the Sun is at its highest point.

Natal Chart*:* This is the astrology chart showing where all the heavenly bodies were at the moment of birth.

Native*:* Traditional astrological term referring to the person or group of people ruled by the sign or house being discussed.

Past Lives*:* Previous lives lived in other bodies, prior to the incarnation in the present body.

How To Use This Book

You will benefit the most from this book if you know your time of birth. However, if you do not have your birth time, using your Sunrise Chart with the Equal House system will also work with the formulas in this book and give you a lot of helpful information. To obtain your free Natal Chart, go to janspiller.com. Click the "time unknown" box if you need a Sunrise Chart.

FINDING YOUR MIDHEAVEN (MC):

The Midheaven is the same thing as the sign ruling your 10th House. Look at your chart printout, locate the abbreviation "MC" in the line-up of planets, and notice the glyph shown to the right. That is the sign of your Midheaven. The printout will also show any planet(s) you have occupying the 10th House. If you need help with the glyphs of the signs and planets, go to janspiller.com and click on "Astrology 101" on the homepage. (My research is based on the Placidus House System, Tropical Zodiac.)

FINDING THE HOUSE CONTAINING YOUR 10TH HOUSE RULER:

The "ruler" of your 10th House is the planet that rules the sign of your Midheaven (or 10th House). Here is the table of equivalents you need to find this information:

If your MC is in:	*The planet ruling your 10th House is:*
Aries	Mars
Taurus	Venus
Gemini	Mercury
Cancer	Moon
Leo	Sun
Virgo	Mercury
Libra	Venus
Scorpio	Pluto
Sagittarius	Jupiter
Capricorn	Saturn
Aquarius	Uranus
Pisces	Neptune

Once you have pinpointed the planet ruling your 10th House, consult your printout and see in which house that planet falls in your chart. For example, if your MC is Cancer, Cancer is ruled by the Moon. In which house does your Moon reside? That is the house containing your 10th House ruler.

FINDING PLANETS LOCATED IN YOUR 10TH HOUSE:

Again, consult your chart printout. There will be a list of planets, the sign they are in, and the house they occupy (refer to the list of symbols below). Notice those planets (if any) that are located in House 10. If you have no planets in House 10 it has special meaning, as well as if you have more than one planet in that House. You can look up the meanings in Chapter 3. Here is a list of the planetary symbols:

Sun	☼	Moon	☽
Mercury	☿	Venus	♀
Mars	♂	Jupiter	♃
Saturn	♄	Uranus	♅
Neptune	♆	Pluto	♇
North Node	☊	South Node	☋

Here is a list of the Sun Sign Symbols:

Aries	♈	Taurus	♉
Gemini	♊	Cancer	♋
Leo	♌	Virgo	♍
Libra	♎	Scorpio	♏
Sagittarius	♐	Capricorn	♑
Aquarius	♒	Pisces	♓

FINDING THE HOUSES RULED BY YOUR 10TH HOUSE PLANETS:

To locate the House(s) ruled by your 10th House planet(s), first look to see which planets (if any) are located in your 10th House. Then use the following table of equivalents to determine which sign that planet rules.

Table of Equivalents:

Sun	Leo
Moon	Cancer
Mercury	Gemini and Virgo

Venus	Taurus and Libra
Mars	Aries
Jupiter	Sagittarius
Saturn	Capricorn
Uranus	Aquarius
Neptune	Pisces
Pluto	Scorpio

For example, if the Moon is located in your 10th House, check your chart to see which of your houses is ruled by Cancer. That is the house ruled by your 10th House planet. If your 10th House planet rules more than one sign, find which house each sign is ruled by. Both represent talents that can help you succeed in the public sector, as well as when you are striving to reach personal goals. For example, if Mercury is located in your 10th House, read the houses ruled by both Gemini and Virgo.

EXAMPLE CHARTS:

To check the accuracy of your calculations, the following charts are included along with their 10th House information.

Bill Gates, born: October 28, 1955, 10:00 pm, Seattle, Washington

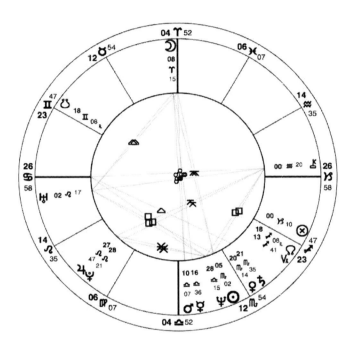

Midheaven - Aries
House containing the 10th House Ruler - House 4
Planet(s) located in the 10th House - Moon
Houses Ruled by 10th House Planet(s) - House 1

Mahatma Gandhi, born: October 2, 1869, 7:12 am, Porbandar, India

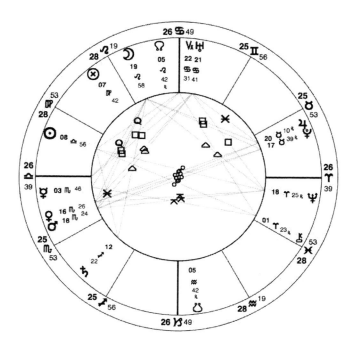

Midheaven - Cancer
House containing the 10th House Ruler - House 10
Planet(s) located in the 10th House - North Node and Moon
Houses Ruled by 10th House Planet(s) - House 10

As an alternative, you can go to janspiller.com and receive a free print out of all your 10th House positions.

CHAPTER 1
KEY TO SUCCESS
Your Midheaven

The Midheaven is the highest point in the astrology chart. If you look at your chart as you would a clock, the sign located at 12:00 is your Midheaven. It represents the way the public sees you. It reveals the style that empowers you to take charge and create success in any aspect of your life. It is the key to being a Manifestor.

The sign on your Midheaven is a compass you can follow. Professionally, it shows the career path that is best suited to you. Personally, these are the traits that need to be integrated and expressed in your personality for you to be successful. They are the qualities that you need to be consciously emphasizing and expressing in relationships to gain success and a position of feeling competent and in charge.

ARIES MIDHEAVEN PEOPLE

CREATING SUCCESS

Aries Midheaven people create successful outcomes when they openly express their own point of view. By revealing the way they would like things to go, they create clarity for others and open the way for them to respond from their own reality. They no longer have to guess about whether they can "be themselves" and still keep the other person on their team. If the other person supports their goal, Aries Midheaven has gained a partner in their work. If not, they haven't wasted their time in trying vainly to enlist the support of someone who inherently has a different value.

It can be scary at first, since Aries Midheaven is so attuned to other people, yet taking the initiative and following their own independent impulses opens them to self-discovery through the process of attaining their goals. The byproduct of their courage is the secure and joyous feeling of being truly in charge of their own life. In relationships as well, letting the other person know what they feel frees them from co-dependencies that weaken their initiative.

Happiness enters into every area of their life that they approach when they directly reveal their intentions, rather than trying to manipulate situations to gain support. Success occurs when they responsibly share with others the direction they would like to go in. By openly revealing their desires to others, they place themselves in charge of their own destiny.

THEIR ACHILLES HEEL

Aries Midheaven people so deeply fear losing the safety of their role as "nice person" that they may never experience the satisfaction of being a person in their own right. Their desire to appear accommodating, diplomatic, and cooperative can keep them from asserting their independence. This stance is a survival tool they developed in childhood that no longer serves them in adult life.

When the pattern is carried into adult life, fearing the loss of others' cooperation may prompt them to constantly accommodate friends, family, and colleagues. Yet this behavior invites disappointment; sacrificing their integrity leads to feeling insufficiently appreciated.

The habit of manipulating others to maintain some identity and to create a harmonious-seeming emotional state leaves little room within a relationship for their true personal feelings. The identity they create is often an extension of others, the "harmony" contrived. Thus they may compromise themselves out of having any personal feelings of their own.

Unhappiness comes through this loss of identity, and through never letting themselves relate deeply and authentically to another person, since that would involve abandoning the security of their social manipulations. As a consequence, others may sense the "wishy-washiness" of their emotional interactions and feel reluctant to relate to them on an intimate level.

SELF-ACTUALIZATION

Happiness enters into every area of their life that the Aries Midheaven person approaches from the standpoint of revealing their own independent energies. When they abandon their preoccupation with pleasing people, they are free to concentrate instead on asserting their true identity. Their independent spirit and pioneering ideas begin to emerge, leading them unerringly to the unabashed joy of experiencing themselves as a person in their own right.

As a byproduct of expressing themselves positively and spontaneously, they create a space into which others can enter of their own accord. Concentrating on being their own leader makes them happy, and simultaneously attracts people who don't need to be manipulated in order to be in a state of harmony with them.

By letting others see them as an entity in their own right, they model the integrity of experiencing and expressing their own feelings. Thus they open themselves to attracting the intimacy and harmonious relationships they have always sought

THEIR "HOME BASE"

Their early environmental conditioning was in many ways very peaceful and beautiful. Harmony was central, and personal compromise for the sake of getting along with family members was emphasized.

Their childhood survival tools included diplomacy, an elegant presence, and an affinity for harmony and beauty. Early on, Aries Midheaven people learned that "keeping the peace" was their key to personal safety. Carried into adult life, however, this can create an over-dependence on partnership and the accord of others that keeps them from finding or following their own path.

Past lives spent in developing strong partnerships as a key to their security are indicated here. The Aries Midheaven person has been a spouse, a partner, the support person for another in situations where the strength of the partnership ensured their own survival. Carried into their present adult life, fear of disrupting the "safety" of the current peace may tempt them to suppress their instinctive responses to people and situations. In this life, it is their instincts that best guide their way.

GOOD CAREER CHOICES

Aries Midheaven people are happiest in professions where they have plenty of room to initiate actions and "do their own thing." They need a career that allows them to independently follow their own impulses in reaching their goals.

Their chief talent lies in being a warrior whose energy and courage lead to the new beginnings that start them off in the right direction. This could be any field where they are required to be a self-starter. Their strong suit is in taking charge and initiating projects, inspiring others to back them up with support.

Self-contentment is assured through allowing the world to see them as a person of integrity. By being honest and direct in saying what they think, the Aries Midheaven person will be perceived as an independent, self-sufficient leader: ambitious, ready to lead the way, and unswayed when their instincts are at odds with social proprieties.

TAURUS MIDHEAVEN PEOPLE

CREATING SUCCESS

Taurus Midheaven people achieve successful outcomes when they openly express their own values. Their profession needs to reflect those values, perhaps by building something that furthers what they feel is a worthy principle. Whatever their chosen career, as they implement their values within it, success will follow.

In every area of their life – profession, relationships, finances – when they freely reveal themselves and what is important to them, they access the serenity and strength of letting others know where they stand. Then they can ask the other person what he or she considers important; if their values match, they have a partner.

It can be scary at first since they are deeply attuned to others' needs and motivations, and they fear alienating them or losing their support. In reality, when they state what is important to them, it becomes easier for them to allow those with differing values to go their own way. Thus, they open the door to those who share their aims.

The natural byproduct of such openness is an empowering feeling of stability, self-esteem, of being in charge of their own destiny. Happiness enters into every area of life where Taurus Midheaven people rise above the need to control others and reorient toward those pursuits that give them a sense of self-direction and self-worth.

THEIR ACHILLES HEEL

Taurus Midheaven people are deeply perceptive of others' values, and fear losing the safety of this "invisible" position. By keeping their perceptions secret and continually altering their values to harmonize with those around them, they may feel that they can manipulate others and remain always in control. While they maintain this position their power cannot be challenged, but neither can it be validated. This stance is a survival tool they developed in childhood that no longer serves them in adult life.

If they concern themselves only with manipulating and maintaining power over those around them, it begins to weaken their sense of personal identity. To regain a feeling of worthiness, they may attempt to control others' perceptions of *them*, thus further isolating themselves from true intimacy with another. People who are originally attracted to them may find "no one home" to relate intimately with. Their habit of self-secrecy thwarts both inner stability and personal identity. Unhappiness results wherever they seek control over others' perceptions.

SELF-ACTUALIZATION

Happiness enters into every area of life where their attention is released from controlling others, and refocused on establishing what *they* consider of value in the world. When relationships are based on the honest disclosure of their own true values, they attract people who value the same things they do. Then they can experience the joy of relating to people who of their own accord are in alignment with them.

When Taurus Midheaven people surround themselves with people whose values are in agreement with their own, they quite naturally support their sense of self-esteem. By openly acknowledging what they have to contribute, Taurus Midheaven people reveal the penetrating quality of their mind. By affirming their values to the world and confidently putting them into practice, they simultaneously enable deeply transformative processes in others. Happiness is ensured through the feelings of self-worth and inner stability that result from openly disclosing to others – in every area of their life – that which they truly value.

THEIR "HOME BASE"

The early environmental conditioning of Taurus Midheaven people was in many ways very disruptive and disturbing to their emotions. It may be that one or both of their parents had a destructive attitude toward the other, or that there were power struggles within the home.

Whatever its specifics, the intensity of their early environment accustomed them to "living on the edge" and familiarized them with crisis. Carried into adult life, this can foster a tendency to respond to unstable situations with a feeling of "home."

Their survival tools included developing the ability to tune in to the values and needs of others in order to maintain their own sense of personal power. They considered their acceptance of and ability to deal with crisis as key to their personal safety.

Past lives spent "living on the edge" due to the power urges of those around them are indicated here. Taurus Midheaven people possess a keen sense of strategy and awareness of the psychology of others, and even now tend to attribute their survival to their ability to navigate successfully within the power structures around them. They are learning that their best security rests in their self-sufficiency in establishing results that they personally build, one step at a time.

GOOD CAREER CHOICES

Taurus Midheaven people are happiest in professions where they have a sense of "building" or creating something that will endure over the long haul. It needs to be an area that is in alignment with their values, so that what they are working toward makes them feel good about themselves. Some of their many talents can include: a gifted voice, artistic abilities, creative involvement in a sensual experience (such as catering, cooking, or massage).

They're happiest when they have room to move at their own speed, according to their own comfort levels. The best fields for them call upon their ability to tap into their qualities of persistence, loyalty, and steadfastness — they have the ability to see things through to the end. Any field that involves money management is suited to their natural talents. When they focus on matters involving finance, they are filled with a positive, balanced energy that empowers them to take charge. Other professions well-suited to their talents include: working with the earth (farming, floral arrangement), sensual involvements (such as massage or other healing forms), and artistic venues where their appreciation of beauty comes into play.

Self-contentment comes through allowing the world to see them as stable, reliable, and materially competent. By relying upon their own efforts and building what they feel comfortable with, they access the happiness of a solid sense of personal self-worth.

GEMINI MIDHEAVEN PEOPLE

CREATING SUCCESS

Gemini Midheaven people achieve successful outcomes when they keep talking! They achieve recognition by openly communicating their own opinions and ideas, and by listening to other people's perspectives- Self-censorship is thus replaced with the healthy disclosure of whatever thoughts and feelings are arising at the moment. Open communication is their key.

It can be scary at first since there are underlying feelings of "not knowing what to say" and the fear that revealing themselves could lead to a loss of freedom. In fact, the opposite is true. When they openly communicate their thoughts and feelings, they gain the freedom to change their mind. Gemini Midheaven people need to keep their communication on a factual – not a theoretical – level. As they share the facts of what they are experiencing, others will be able to "hear" them better. Asking questions and gaining more information from others gives them the data they need to find logical solutions that work for everyone.

This exchange of information is invigorating for them! "Truth" – on the level of daily relationships – is simply a willingness to disclose their genuine perceptions and feelings, rather than stifle them in the hope that somehow silence will resolve the situation. In personal relationships, communicating without self-censoring is their key to success. When in doubt, don't get quiet – get chatty! Pick up the phone and start the communication ball rolling.

Happiness enters into every area of their life where they replace an attitude of "being right" with the simple joy of sharing different perspectives and ideas.

THEIR ACHILLES HEEL

Gemini Midheaven people have a fear of losing the safety of their role as "the teacher," of releasing their perennial, purposeful, philosophical perspective on "the way things are." This stance of righteousness leads others to put little stock in their lofty thoughts. This stance is a survival tool they developed in childhood that no longer serves them in adult life. To be secure in their inner foundation, they may feel the need for others to concede that they are "right" in their perception of life. An urge to prove their intellectual superiority can launch them into philosophical battles in which nobody wins.

Conversely, when they cannot justify negative emotions as being "right" in their belief system, they may withhold what they are really thinking or feeling. When excessive pride keeps them from communicating their insecurities and upsets, this appearance of aloofness creates insecurity in those who wish to relate to them on intimate levels.

As a consequence, they believe their security is based on being able to account for every aspect of their behavior within their belief system, on justifying their ideas and actions by the "rightness" of their philosophy. This self-righteous stance creates a ponderous feeling that is difficult for even them to bear, and a sense of being isolated from others by their basic outlook.

SELF-ACTUALIZATION

Happiness enters into every area of their life where they replace "being right" with an attitude of openness to and enjoyment of differing perspectives and ideas. Curiosity is their friend. Their best communication is based on lightness and an easy sharing of thoughts that spontaneously occur to them. Then cheerfulness enters their life, along with an ease in keeping the current of verbal exchanges with others flowing back and forth. Letting go of the need to "be right" before revealing their thoughts and ideas leaves them free to communicate fully with others.

Gemini Midheaven people become teachers through their willingness to share ideas with others even though they may not, in advance, have been aware of what information they gained from them. Thus they allow others (and themselves) to learn and grow. Factual communication, far from depriving them of their freedom, confers the ability to change their mind.

Ease and joy enter every area of their life where they are willing to welcome fresh new perspectives, where they maintain openness and non-attachment to expressing the thoughts that occur to them in diverse situations. Happiness comes from relating to all sorts of people, familiar and unfamiliar, taking interest in *their* ideas and perspectives. Social ease ensues as a byproduct of the spontaneous communication of their thoughts – without attachment or investment in them, or the need to "be right" – in response to existing and emerging situations.

THEIR "HOME BASE"

Gemini Midheaven's early environmental conditioning was in many ways very positive and expansive, prompting them to exercise the freedom to pursue their own path to truth. Abundance, in some way, was part of the picture. Quite probably, one of their parents seemed "bigger than life."

There may have been strong beliefs and philosophies in their family about "how life is," including who *they* should be and what they should be doing. Perhaps there was a moralistic element to things, leading to their belief in adult life that in order to be "safe," they have to be "right." In some ways, communication may have been censored so that only certain kinds of conversation were acceptable. This carries forward into adult life as a reticence to openly communicate with others, out of fear that their thoughts may be unacceptable or invalidated.

Spiritual and religious past lives are indicated here, as well as a natural feeling of good luck due to Life itself supporting them. They have an innate optimism, a positive attitude, and an abiding trust that somehow, some way, things will work out just fine.

GOOD CAREER CHOICES

Gemini Midheaven people are happiest in a career where they can communicate ideas. This could be writing, teaching, publishing, sales, or marketing. Gemini also relates to fields involving the internet and spreading information through the media.

They do best in a profession where their opportunity to grow intellectually is unlimited. Their most satisfying profession is one that requires the use of logic, fact-gathering, and information-sharing. As a "people" person, they can tap into their flirtatious qualities, enjoy being in the moment, and lighten the mood of others.

Self-contentment is assured through allowing the world to see them as interested and interesting, cheerful and able to lightheartedly relate to a multiplicity of challenges, people, and situations.

CANCER MIDHEAVEN PEOPLE

CREATING SUCCESS

Cancer Midheaven people achieve successful outcomes when they express themselves with an awareness of others' feelings. They feel empowered by a position of caring about other people. Their concern for the lives of others opens the way for them to support them and achieve their own aims as well.

It can be scary at first, since Cancer Midheaven people learned to be somewhat hard-hearted and tough in childhood. And yet, speaking in terms of feelings magically opens the doors to whatever they want in life. Asking others how they are feeling, and wanting to nurture and support them, encourages others to be interested in hearing about their own vulnerabilities and feelings.

Ironically, by giving up control, they gain a true sense of being in charge of their own destiny.

THEIR ACHILLES HEEL

Cancer Midheaven people fear losing the safety of their role as the perennial "authority," always sufficient unto themselves. They may also avoid allowing themselves to be emotionally vulnerable for fear of losing the security of having total control over their own life. This stance is a survival tool they developed in childhood that no longer serves them in adult life. It leads to the unhappiness of self-isolation, of remaining so rigidly in control that they allow no one to interact with them on a deep level.

If they seek to relate only to people and situations that they can dominate or use in some way, they will find themselves very often alone, alienated from others by endless justifications of the rightness of their position. This defensive position precludes interaction on a deep emotional level and can deter others from desiring to establish intimate contact with them. The result is the disappointing experience of gaining the respect of no one.

SELF-ACTUALIZATION

Happiness enters into every area of their life where rigid rules of behavior are replaced with an attitude of wanting to share themselves and care for other people. They "win" by being willing to relate with others on an emotional level, by letting them see their vulnerability, their humanness, and the truth (as opposed to the drama) of what they experience in their deepest nature. As they allow themselves to be vulnerable, they automatically gain the respect of others.

The Cancer Midheaven person's willingness to openly communicate their feelings and vulnerabilities inspires others to organize their own emotional lives. Happiness comes through relating to others equally, without sorting them by their rank or usefulness to their purposes. Joy enters into every area of life that is approached with an attitude of openness to emotional change and a maternal protectiveness of others' sensitivities.

THEIR "HOME BASE"

Their early environmental conditioning was in many ways very restrictive and one of their parents was more authority figure than caregiver. Essentially, they were programmed, learning early on who they should be when they grew up, the job they should have, the person they should marry. This carries over in their adult life as a feeling that they must always be on top of their emotions, that vulnerability is not permitted, that safety depends upon being always in control.

Their survival tools included taking responsibility for creating successes that would engender self-respect. They learned to rely on themselves as the authority in their life, to ensure their own safety. In childhood, confusingly, they were in some way handed the responsibility for family success long before they had developed the maturity to know how to take on this role without limiting themselves.

Past lives spent being the person in charge are indicated here, as well as a history of taking personal responsibility for the outcomes in their life. Deep down, there can be a feeling of restriction, a conviction that they must always put duty first, even when that comes at the expense of what nourishes them. Cancer Midheaven people are learning to rise above the need to control in lieu of having caring, nurturing relationships with others.

GOOD CAREER CHOICES

Cancer Midheaven people are happiest in careers that allow them to nurture others, to express empathy and concern. They want the personal, emotional involvement to be a part of their livelihood. Anything involving the home — real estate, interior decorating, cooking, care-taking — works best for them. This extends to working with peoples' home base — i.e., their foundation, whether it be physical, mental, emotional, or spiritual

Cancer Midheaven's most successful goals result in providing a sense of personal safety for all involved. Their specialties are their awareness of others' feelings and the ability to draw upon a mothering quality within themselves to lend support and encouragement to others. Their greatest career fulfillment will be accompanied by a sense of family in their interactions with colleagues.

Self-contentment is assured when they allow the world to see them as a loving person, deeply caring and sensitive to others' emotions; and when they share the unusual strength and integrity of their own feelings.

LEO MIDHEAVEN PEOPLE

CREATING SUCCESS

Leo Midheaven people achieve successful outcomes when they allow themselves to become fully involved in creating results that are important to them. This process includes listening to other people's responses. When they are not receiving the feedback they desire, it is important to be willing to change their presentation slightly, perhaps by approaching from a different angle. The information they gain as others respond to their "script" is an invaluable resource that can help them more directly reach their goals.

A comedian onstage knows the value of creating results! By listening for which jokes get the longest, loudest laughs, then tailoring subsequent performances to what delighted the audience best, he or she moves toward success. Just so, when Leo Midheaven people are willing to take center stage and match their presentation to the needs of their chosen audience, they will create the results they want and experience the joy of being in charge of their own destiny.

It can be scary at first, since childhood conditioning prompted them to equate personal safety with "going with the flow" instead of pursuing what *they* wanted. In their adult life, this childhood strategy does not serve them well. But as they fully involve themselves in creating the results they want, they will engender the commitment they need to use others' feedback to fine-tune their method and successfully reach their goal.

Happiness enters into every area of their life where they replace detachment with a dramatic, inspiring display of emotions to let others know how they feel and what they want.

THEIR ACHILLES HEEL

Leo Midheaven people fear losing the safety of their emotionally detached and objective outlook on life. This stance is a survival tool they developed in childhood that no longer serves them in adult life.

This impersonal approach to the emotions can lead to the dry disappointment of not being able to experience the joys of an intimate relationship.

Their objective, knowledgeable stance can negatively impact others. When they base their decisions exclusively on detached, intellectual ideals and unemotional appraisals, they may create tremendous emotional upheaval and drama around them without ever understanding the cause.

This behavior thwarts the fulfillment of an intimate relationship, because when others get close to them, they feel unsafe and withdraw. Approaching others from an aloof, superior base leads to unhappiness.

SELF-ACTUALIZATION

Happiness enters into every area of life where detachment gives way to the dramatic, inspiring display of genuine and positive emotions! When they no longer allow their intellect to dictate to their feelings, they are free to express their emotions clearly and compellingly. At last they can experience the joy and excitement of projecting their love in a way that communicates "love" to others!

In intimate relationships and every human interchange, when they make clear what *they* want, they open the door for others to follow suit; then all involved can work out a fair solution. As Leo Midheaven people allow their emotions to find their own generous expression and approach others warmly with their heart instead of their head, people become more open and receptive to them.

When Leo Midheaven people directly communicate loyalty, trust, passion, and warm acceptance, they inspire the same in others. And by releasing the need to be forever detached and knowledgeable, they gain access to the entire range of their emotions. This new, compelling level of self-expression imparts their knowledge to others as a natural byproduct. It also gives them an objective perspective in their lives, as it introduces them to the joys of free, spontaneous self-expression.

THEIR "HOME BASE"

Their early environmental conditioning was in many ways very cool and detached. Their parents were so burdened by tasks and responsibilities that it was difficult for them to see Leo Midheaven as an individual in their own right. They weren't recognized and appreciated for their specialness. Thus in adult life their habit is to withdraw from the spotlight, to go along with what others want, rather than bring their own individual gifts into play.

Their survival tools included the ability to go with the flow and to consider the whole picture, rather than just their personal preferences. In some ways, they were never fully able to experience being a child.

Past lives spent within strong group bonds are indicated here, along with a tendency to look beyond their desires to the bigger picture of what is good for all involved. There is also a tendency to put others on a pedestal, to yield to others' Light rather than stepping forward to display their own. Yet in this life, it is precisely through displaying their individual gifts and feelings that happiness is their natural reward.

GOOD CAREER CHOICES

Leo Midheaven people are happiest in a profession that allows them to express their creative talents! They are gifted in fields involving children, the entertainment industry, and creative endeavors of all sorts. Being onstage is certainly an area where they can shine. They need to feel like a "star" in their own world.

In their profession, they are at their best when there's plenty of room for them to draw upon their qualities of strength, leadership, determination, and enthusiasm. To achieve the greatest happiness in their career, they must feel that their innate creativity can continue to grow and be expressed.

Self-contentment is theirs when they allow the world to see them as a person of power, creativity, forthright expression, and emotional generosity.

VIRGO MIDHEAVEN PEOPLE

CREATING SUCCESS

Virgo Midheaven people achieve successful outcomes when they focus on their intended goal and carefully plan how they will get there. Analyzing the details of a situation, making a realistic time schedule, and sticking to their routine no matter what – these are their keys to manifesting their goals and feeling in charge of their life. Routines are vital for them, and so is writing out a list of what they intend to accomplish each day. These essential tools will help them stay focused and on course.

It can be scary at first since they are so sensitive and attuned to helping other people with their troubles. They tend to equate their basic safety with their ability to go with the flow of life and events. But by making a plan and sticking to it no matter what, they rise above any feelings of helplessness. Empowered with a sense of creating their own destiny, they can enter into relationships with confidence, ready to make a plan that serves both parties. As long as they fulfill their part of the plan, a person in accord will keep up his or her commitment. Anyone not in harmony with the plan had best be on their way so someone more dependable can enter their life.

THEIR ACHILLES HEEL

Virgo Midheaven people fear losing the safety of their role as a tender, compassionate victim, in contact with the "cosmic whole" yet unable to organize themselves here on Earth. This stance is a survival tool they developed in childhood that no longer serves them in adult life. By refusing to focus or define their direction, they become less visible to others; they experience the unhappiness of nobody really noticing their plight or benefiting from their spiritual vision.

They may seek sympathy from others, hoping they will recognize their basic goodness and accept and love them unconditionally. In reality, this approach leads to disappointment, as people are not inspired to relate to them deeply. Isolated through the helplessness of their basic outlook, they feel misunderstood – a martyr. They may also isolate themselves from true intimacy through an unwillingness to see their ideals of love take any physical form. As a consequence, they may find themselves dissatisfied, unhappy, and disillusioned with life.

SELF-ACTUALIZATION

Happiness enters into every area where a stance of "cosmic helplessness" is replaced by an attitude of down-to-earth *helpfulness* in the lives of others. By releasing utopian fantasies, they free themselves to envision a new ideal of service, one based upon their ability to practically apply it. They can then experience the unparalleled joy that accompanies being an active participant in bringing their spiritual vision alive in the here and now!

When Virgo Midheaven people focus and begin to act – doing the small services that they see are needful and within their reach, no matter how mundane – they experience the joy of materially acting upon their vision. As a natural byproduct of this practical service, those whom they serve on any level also get a sense of the wholeness of their vision; they are no longer afraid of being pulled into a bottomless void. Thus, through their willingness to rise up and take an active part in putting into practice their spiritual ideals, they create room in their life for others to relate to them on an intimate, highly personal, satisfying level.

Happiness comes into any area of their life where they are willing to see their ideals manifested in physical form and do their part to bring their ideal of cosmic love into a practical, material application. Having a routine, a schedule of how they use their time, and adopting other helpful habits gives them the structure and the confidence they need to vigorously approach their goals, and the satisfaction that comes from reaching them.

THEIR "HOME BASE"

Their early environmental conditioning was in many ways very confusing and disorienting. Chaos was part of the picture. To ensure their personal survival it was necessary to simply go along with whatever was happening. In many ways, their capacity to create order was undermined through lack of encouragement. Deep feelings of helplessness may have resulted.

Consequently, their survival tools included developing the ability to be very understanding and forgiving of other people's shortcomings, which may be expressed in their adult life as a lack of discrimination. The Virgo Midheaven person may also have a tendency to give up too easily or to allow a myriad of outside influences to distract them from their own path. They can become so adaptable to constantly changing outer circumstances that they simply flow along, doing what they can to smooth away distracting influences.

Past lifetimes spent in non-worldly environments are indicated here. They have been in settings that protected them from the world. Monasteries or other physically isolated places provided them with abundant time for self-reflection and self-purification. Hence there is a certain shyness and aloneness deep in their nature. In this life, their deep self-reflection can be expanded to include helping others to become more aware of their own self-sabotaging behaviors. This frees them from feelings of isolation.

GOOD CAREER CHOICES

Virgo Midheaven people are happiest in a profession where they feel they are being of real service to others. A healing profession would be ideal, such as a physician, nurse, holistic practitioner, dentist, or spiritual advisor. They would also be content in a field that utilizes their ability for organization.

Their calling is to bring order out of chaos. They are very gifted at detailed work. A career that involves careful handling and study would stimulate their feelings of competency and satisfaction. Their best career choice would also involve their ability for analysis and practical planning, a talent that brings clarity to one and all.

Self-contentment is assured through allowing the world to see them as effective, attentive to detail, realistic, hard-working, diligent, and practical in implementing their spiritual ideals.

LIBRA MIDHEAVEN PEOPLE

CREATING SUCCESS

Libra Midheaven people achieve successful outcomes when they link with another in a partnership effort. Their ideal profession will involve one-on-one dealings with another person, whether that other is their business partner or their client in a counseling situation. In every area of life that they approach as a team player seeking cooperation and mutual support – career, relationships, finances – they will gain the confidence of feeling in charge of their own destiny.

True partnership is not a co-dependent relationship, it is based on *interdependency*. Each person brings to the table their own separate identity and contributes that in a cooperative effort toward team goals. Partnership is the key to Libra Midheaven's individual success, and questioning others about their goals in life will yield the information they need to see whether the other person's objectives fit with their own.

It can be scary at first, since they believe that following their own independent impulses is their key to success and survival. Yet, if the other person's goals match well with theirs, when Libra Midheaven adds their innate courage and strength to the mix it can create a highly successful team! Happiness enters every area of life where they seek balance and harmony through the open sharing of feelings, and allow the needs of others to fairly influence their actions.

THEIR ACHILLES HEEL

Libra Midheaven people fear losing the safety of their role as the impulsive, independent, self-reliant person who always goes his or her own way. This stance is a survival tool they developed in childhood that no longer serves them in adult life. By failing to consider other people's needs before making decisions, they open themselves to unhappiness, since others in turn may not support their actions.

Their habit is to act based on their needs alone, a "me first" attitude that is alienating to others. When others cannot trust them to consider their feelings, Libra Midheaven may find themselves cut off from the joys of deeply intimate relationships. Spending their energy on endless conquests without deep or sustaining benefit to themselves or others yields emptiness over the long haul.

The result of such thoughtless and rash expressions of personal identity, oriented only to winning their personal desires, is the disappointment of others neither understanding nor acknowledging their capabilities or positive strengths. Thus the "security" of maintaining their identity is created at the expense of discouraging others from wanting to relate to them on a deep level.

SELF-ACTUALIZATION

Happiness enters into every area of life where they expand their "me first" attitude to include other people on their winning team. Awareness of others' needs and desires then empowers them to use their gift for taking the initiative in a way that leads to cooperation between all parties involved.

Joy comes through the realization that only when *everyone* wins are they able to achieve a true victory. Gentleness and concern take root in their nature as they strive to create harmony in intimate relationships and to consistently consider other people's feelings. Seeing this approach on their part inspires their mate and partners to trust them and to relate to them on the deepest levels of emotional intimacy. This opens the way for them to experience the personal peace and lasting happiness of a harmonious relationship.

Happiness enters every area of the Libra Midheaven person's life where they seek to understand another's singular identity, both by asking them questions and by observing and acknowledging their unique characteristics. By considering the goals of others as well as their own to make fair decisions for action, they create an empowering balance and harmony for themselves and those around them.

THEIR "HOME BASE"

Libra Midheaven's early environmental conditioning was in many ways very supportive of their independence, geared toward their becoming strong in their own right. They were given abundant attention within a family situation that empowered them to grow and develop on their own. They were happily "their own person" at a very young age.

Their survival tools included learning to take care of themselves; of necessity, they developed personal courage and assertiveness. The urge to take chances and the desire to discover themselves resonate strongly in their inner nature. They have consequently made choices in their adult life that are "gutsy" from their family's point of view.

Past lives spent on their own – perhaps as a warrior or the initiator of a new idea – are indicated here. In such times their independence was an inspiration to others; as a result, they are likely to possess an inner feeling of bravery and self-confidence and the ability to pave their own way through life. This is accompanied by an innocence and being willing to discover themselves through whatever situation befalls them. That being said, the key to their success lies in partnering with another

GOOD CAREER CHOICES

Libra Midheaven people are happiest in professions where they can relate to others on a one-to-one basis. Peace, harmony, and fairness are important values to them, and any profession that aims for those qualities is very suited to their nature. Thus they could be a diplomat, a mediator, or a person who introduces beauty into the environment, such as a home decorator.

Beauty and equilibrium are important to them and need to be considered in choosing the right profession. Uniting in partnership is essential to their professional success. This could mean working with a business partner, or some form of counseling or consulting work in which their aim is to support the other person's efforts to reach to their goals.

Self-contentment is assured through allowing the world to see them as charming, humorous, diplomatic, and able to reach conclusions that are fair to all concerned. They gain self-respect and evoke the respect of others when they use their natural abilities to be objective in their outlook, balanced in their dealings, and just in their decisions: in short, to be a likable person who plays fair with others.

SCORPIO MIDHEAVEN PEOPLE

CREATING SUCCESS

Scorpio Midheaven people achieve successful outcomes when they link with a powerful partner. Through their wholehearted efforts to support him or her, they are transformed and empowered, blossoming into an expanded sense of self and possibility. Exploring other people's goals can show them the next partner to link with; an innate sense of excitement about their aims will be their signal!

This can be scary for them at first, since they are attuned to believing that their survival depends upon preserving the status quo. They are comfortable with things just as they are; to go in a new direction – even (or perhaps especially) an exciting direction – can feel intimidating and risky. Yet when they find the courage to embrace the risk, link with a partner, and take a fresh path, they open themselves not only to change but to empowerment and self-renewal.

For them, the byproduct of this kind of risk-taking is the joy of feeling in charge of their own destiny. Happiness enters into every area of their life in which they are willing to actively choose change over the status quo.

THEIR ACHILLES HEEL

Scorpio Midheaven natives fear losing their position as a practical person with solid, reliable material values. Yet the image projected is boring and the cost of maintaining it is exorbitant; within its confines they may never reach beyond their own values to understand what is of worth to others.

The result is the loneliness of not having their *own* worth validated by others.

They may stubbornly maintain fixed beliefs about what is important in life. This stance is a survival tool they developed in childhood that no longer serves them in adult life. This can lead to the strain of feeling continually on the defensive as they struggle to uphold their own position against other people's power, which they perceive as threatening. One natural result of this defensive stance is their growing conviction of their own powerlessness.

If Scorpio Midheaven people continue approaching life with a stubborn resistance to change, they will be deprived of the comfort and support of deep intimacy and meaningful emotional sharing with another. By getting too close, they may find themselves changing; thus they may build thick protective walls around what they most value. This defensive attitude may work only too well, alienating prospective partners or allies from attempting intimacy with them, or even from being around them for long. Far from creating admiration, others may perceive their basic beliefs as stodgy and static, and fear being "bogged down" in them!

SELF-ACTUALIZATION

Happiness enters every area of their life where they relinquish intolerance and strive instead to recognize and explore what others consider valuable. Perceiving others' motivations and merging with them - that is, sharing perceptions to create a third perspective - enhances their own sense of value as well as that of others. By moving out of their comfort zone to pursue and establish their true personal power, they can experience the joy of relating to others in significant ways.

By fully engaging in this process, they allow themselves to encompass internal changes, and in their willingness to experience personal transformation, they are empowered. Happiness enters every area of their life where they relinquish intolerance and expand their self-reflective abilities to include reflection on the merits of others.

THEIR "HOME BASE"

Scorpio Midheaven's early environment was in many ways safe, dependable, and comfortable; a place in which they could count on loyalty and support. Money was not scarce and they are likely to have been provided with all the physical necessities of life. They were taught strong family values, including persistence, ownership, and self-reliance.

Their survival tools included loyalty to family members, a willingness to proceed step by step to achieve results that would last, and a natural affinity for money. Thus, as an adult, they equate their survival with personal comfort and financial stability.

Past lives that focused on a comfortable lifestyle and the accumulation of tangible assets are indicated here, shedding light on their strong attachment to material values. In this life, however, it is their willingness to step "outside the box" of their fixed beliefs that brings happiness and access to personal power.

GOOD CAREER CHOICES

Scorpio Midheaven people are happiest in professions where they have a sense of living on the edge, taking a chance — either by being involved in politics, psychology, or a job where the concepts of power and control motivate them. Crisis situations stimulate a feeling of competency in them, and their talent in dealing with such situations is a true asset in their career.

They are happiest in professions that emphasize change, rather than maintaining the status quo. Having a business partner whose values resonate with their own is essential to their success. They have an incredible ability to support and empower others to reach their worldly aims, and Scorpio Midheaven is able to rouse others to go through the personal transformations necessary to claim their own potency.

Self-contentment comes when they allow the world to see them as ready to change and grow and willing to take both psychological and material risks in order to do so – as deeply perceptive in their relationships, and powerful by virtue of their ability to handle personal intensity.

SAGITTARIUS MIDHEAVEN PEOPLE

CREATING SUCCESS

Sagittarius Midheaven people achieve successful outcomes when they choose personal freedom over acceptance by others. When they put ethics and morality first, their rewards are peace of mind and a trust in positive outcomes.

Finding solutions is invigorating for them! Their active mind can logically bounce back and forth until an epiphany occurs, and suddenly the answer they were seeking becomes apparent and clear. When they align themselves with walking the high road, they gain an optimistic view, a trusting connection with positive spiritual forces, the courage to take chances, and the faith that Life will take care of them.

It can be scary at first since subconsciously Sagittarius Midheaven people equate their personal survival with being in mental accord with others. Yet when they take a stand for truth as they see it, their need for validation by others recedes as if by magic. Speaking directly from their own truth frees everyone involved to make the individual decisions that serve them best. Seeing life as an adventure empowers them to take risks and leads them to an ever-increasing appreciation of its scope and possibilities. Foreign travel, whether physical or through expanding their consciousness into new realms, enhances their self-authority.

Happiness enters into every area of Sagittarius Midheaven's life where an attitude of playful superficiality is replaced by the earnest desire for honest, direct communication. This straightforwardness yields both peace of mind, and a deeper understanding of any situation that life presents them.

THEIR ACHILLES HEEL

Sagittarius Midheaven people fear losing the security they feel when relating to and loosely identifying with a variety of people and ideas, and the safety of their role as "Mr. or Ms. Jack of All Trades." This stance is a survival tool they developed in childhood that no longer serves them in adult life. Lack of focus can be their downfall; it invites the unhappiness of being thought "scattered" and not taken seriously by others.

By attempting to communicate with everyone, they diffuse their basic internal energies, allowing many often conflicting viewpoints to enter as if they were their own. This attachment to variety – and the fear of losing it – may cause them to forego the nourishment of a deeply intimate relationship, fearing the loss of variety it would require. Their superficial attitude may repel others from wanting to draw close. Thus the consequence of holding on to their role as the "perpetual, curious child" is the personal unhappiness of not penetrating beyond the surface of any area of life.

SELF-ACTUALIZATION

Happiness enters into those areas of life where flirtatious superficiality is replaced by the earnest desire to gain a larger perspective. Wherever and whenever they maintain this focus, their intuition is activated. Relying on philosophical or religious overviews for solutions gives Sagittarius Midheaven people access to the strength and stability of the collected mental-emotional energies within these systems.

Discrimination is key for them; by lifting their attention from life's endless trivialities to seek broad philosophical solutions, they experience the joy and authentic security born of firm mental purpose. And by traveling the high road of ethics, morality, and truth, they both respect themselves and gain the respect of others.

THEIR "HOME BASE"

Sagittarius Midheaven's early environmental conditioning was in many ways filled with trickery and the mental manipulations of people around them. They had to develop high intelligence at a young age in order to cope with the intrigue that surrounded them. Thus in their adult life, there is a tendency to be attracted to manipulative people as they remind them of "home."

Their survival tools included a fast-thinking mind and an ability to see things from other people's points of view. In their early life, these skills ensured their safety by helping them outsmart the rampant games in their environment. In adult life, however, this can lead to being so hyper-aware of others that they lose track of their own truth.

Past lives as students and teachers are indicated here, making it all too easy for them to fall into the role of perpetual student in the here and now – that is, to choose continual learning. However, in this life, success and satisfaction come when they demonstrate and share what they have learned, inspiring others with their own active example.

GOOD CAREER CHOICES

Sagittarius Midheaven people are happiest in professions that involve a lot of personal freedom. This could be a field involving foreign travel, import/export business, or adventure tours. They have an innate desire to inspire others to reach beyond their limitations and discover something new. Depending upon their interests, they could also be a great religious leader or an inspirational speaker.

For them to be happy in their career, they need to feel that there's a component of inspiration in it… an acknowledgment of the higher principles of ethics, law, and a trust in a beneficent cosmic order. Sagittarius Midheaven's natural optimism and belief in positive outcomes are the assets they bring to the table. Their job choice also must provide plenty of room for them to express their spontaneity and follow their sense of adventure. They are happiest in professions that emphasize expansion, rather than staying within logical limits.

Self-contentment is assured through allowing the world to see them as serious thinkers and seekers of philosophical truth; holding noble and inspiring aims; concerned with integrity, morality, and ethics; and ready to teach and inspire others through sharing their larger perspective of life.

CAPRICORN MIDHEAVEN PEOPLE

CREATING SUCCESS

Capricorn Midheaven people achieve successful outcomes when they rise above emotional situations, take charge, and become the CEO. It is key for them to both set a goal and ensure that it is accomplished. For example, if their objective is to bring a domestic matter into greater order, their willingness to direct the situation, without being diverted by sub-dramas, is the approach that will lead to success. Integrity, honoring their commitments, and keeping their word are crucial! Their willingness to take responsibility opens the way for self-respect and earns the respect of others.

This can be scary for them at first, since they are so deeply attuned to the emotions around them that they equate their safety – and their success – with the uninterrupted emotional interdependency of their "family." But seeing others as responsible for their success is profoundly disempowering for them. When they rise above that conviction of dependency, they are free to achieve their goals with or without the support of others, to responsibly manage people and situations in order to reach a common goal. The natural byproduct of their willingness to take charge is the secure and joyous feeling of being in charge of their own life.

Happiness enters into every area of their life where Capricorn Midheaven's attitude of personal vulnerability, neediness, and dependence on others is replaced with an attitude of personal *authority*, responsibility, and the willingness to honor their commitments.

THEIR ACHILLES HEEL

Capricorn Midheaven people cling to their "safe" role as dependent, emotionally sensitive, and vulnerable. They avoid establishing their own direction in life, not wanting to risk losing the dependability and warmth of close family attachments. This stance is a survival tool they developed in childhood that no longer serves them in adult life.

It invites the unhappiness of not feeling truly capable or in control of their own destiny, since they are constantly at the mercy of the whims and moods of those close to them.

When Capricorn Midheaven people maintain a position of extreme sensitivity and defenselessness, they open themselves to the disappointment of other people "letting them down" as they attempt to gain emotional breathing space. Their need to possess those close to them in order to feel secure may cause others to pull away from the limiting, stifling closeness they demand. Thus their yearning for the security of this total – and unwittingly smothering – attachment may bring only frustration as their own need to protect others' individuality repels them from drawing close.

SELF-ACTUALIZATION

Happiness enters into every area of Capricorn Midheaven's life where the willingness to take responsibility for the direction of their life and create joy within it replaces this attitude of personal vulnerability, dependence on others, and emotional neediness. An attitude of personal authority is key to their success—both personal and professional.

Personal joy is theirs for the taking when they cease to perceive their security as based on whether or not those close to them care for them. That is, when they begin to accept their responsibility as the authority within their own life, and the author of it. They will gain the respect and caring of those close to them, not by conscious design but as a natural byproduct of their willingness to serve as an example of responsibility in the world.

Capricorn Midheaven's willingness to attain self-sufficiency will empower them to release the tight emotional holds they have imposed in their intimate relationships. This allows people the room to be truly themselves, and to lose their fear of being emotionally available to them. Others can allow themselves to draw close without risking the destruction of their individual purposes. They experience happiness in any area of their life where instead of attempting to monopolize others' emotions, they focus their energies on attaining their own goals and on being the kind of person that others can look up to.

THEIR "HOME BASE"

Capricorn Midheaven's early environment was in many ways very caring and protective; they learned early on that the family unit was key to their personal safety and survival. Carried into adult life, however, this can lead to a fear of venturing outside the family to position themselves in the larger world.

Their survival tools included a hyper-awareness of other people's emotional states, since their home environment, though protective, was moody and unstable in the sense of lacking unconditional love. Family members had to do things in a certain way to be well-thought-of and to avoid emotional upsets within the family group. Consequently, in their adult life, they may dread the idea of someone close to them becoming upset, and thus allow the upsets of others to distract them from their own path.

Past lives spent developing emotional sensitivity to both themselves and others are indicated here. Thus in this life they are blessed with abundant empathy and the ability to take others' feelings into account when expressing themselves.

GOOD CAREER CHOICES

Capricorn Midheaven's best bet for professional happiness is to hold a position where they are the boss. When they are the CEO, everyone wins. They know how to organize others to meet a common goal because they have a natural business sense. They excel in positions of management, where they are organizing others to produce results.

Their best professional choices will activate their ability to take charge and be responsible for creating successful outcomes. They know how to operate in a situation in which sensible business practices prevail. They have a natural sense of the "pecking order" and are not hesitant to step to the front of the line and assume the position that earns them respect and status.

Self-contentment is assured through allowing the world to see them as worthy of respect: responsible, organized, competent, in control of their own life, and able to manage a variety of situations to the best possible, mutually beneficial outcomes.

AQUARIUS MIDHEAVEN PEOPLE

CREATING SUCCESS

Aquarius Midheaven people achieve successful outcomes when they link with peers who are dedicated to the same ideals and life goals as they are. Their profession is satisfying when it reflects their aim to offer a unique gift to humankind, one that will benefit everyone. In the workplace, when they take "fairness to all" as their guiding principle, they will achieve success.

In every area of their life – profession, finances, and relationships – when they focus on the "big picture" of what others want and need, they are empowered to work with them in ways that further others' life goals as well as their own. And, since their planning has taken the other person's passions into account, others will more readily cooperate with them to create mutual success.

This can be scary at first because Aquarius Midheaven people are so attuned to the drama of creatively expressing themselves – solo! They derive a sense of safety and belonging from their own passionate energy, and equate this with personal survival. Yet when they adopt a *dis*passionate point of view and factor the input of others into their aims, their chances of success soar, since they will then have a perspective wide enough to understand how to create a win-win outcome for everyone.

Happiness enters every area of Aquarius Midheaven's life where, with friendship and unbiased awareness, they take into account the life-dreams of others. This objective awareness of their needs will empower them to link with people who share their aims. When all involved are moving toward one innately shared goal, they can fully reside in the feeling of being in charge of their own destiny.

THEIR ACHILLES HEEL

Aquarius Midheaven people restrict themselves to only a small number of intimates, fearing that by reaching further they might lose the dependability of at least these few reliable sources of love. This stance is a survival tool they developed in childhood that no longer serves them in adult life. It leads to the unhappiness – and insecurity – of not finding the caliber of loyalty in others that they are seeking.

Indulging in dramatic emotional displays that force others to "prove" their allegiance and loyalty by giving them their way can lead instead to self-isolation; no one wants to get close enough to be "blown away" by the intensity of their drama. Aquarius Midheaven people can alienate others with unreasonable personal demands, then wonder why no one measures up to their standards of loyalty or love. This process leads to the unhappiness of feeling unable to move beyond personal drama into a real and satisfying experience of truly loving.

SELF-ACTUALIZATION

Happiness enters into every area of their life where they release unrealistic expectations about romantic love and their demands for personal acceptance and importance, and aim instead for an objective perception of human nature. Wherever Aquarius Midheaven upholds standards of unbiased awareness, ensuring an unwavering flow of love, the larger meaning will be intuitively revealed, and the path to successful action through cooperation with others made clear.

Aquarius Midheaven people achieve success in those relationships which they approach objectively, accepting others as equals able to do their unique part in furthering shared life dreams. When they truly dedicate themselves to humanitarian rather than personal aims, discarding ego's demands for attention and concentrating instead on the accomplishment of group aims, they will attract to themselves peers of similar ideals and open themselves to the joys of participating equally in a team effort.

There is a thrill in recognizing other people's abilities to contribute. By acknowledging their talents, Aquarius Midheaven experiences – as a byproduct, rather than by conscious design – the personal recognition they have always sought. As they expand their foundation of love to encompass love for all their fellow beings, they create sufficient freedom in their emotional system to attract a relationship that supports them.

Their challenge is to exorcise their unrealistic standards of loyalty from their personal relationships and seek instead to expand and fulfill their own highest ideals of loving. By viewing others from a base of understanding, tolerance, and compassion, they will experience the joys of emotional stability and a consistent flow of love.

THEIR "HOME BASE"

Aquarius Midheaven people's early environmental conditioning was in many ways on the dramatic side! While the drama was often rather unpleasant and far from reassuring to a child, as a result of what they experienced they developed a strong will, tremendous self-confidence, and a sense of personal strength.

They developed survival tools that included perfecting their innate abilities to give love to others and to entertain, and calling upon those abilities frequently. Thus in their adult life they are quite comfortable in taking the stage and being the center of attention in their family group.

Aquarius Midheaven people have had past lives spent in cheering up others! As a result, they are likely to be blessed with an innate, persistent feeling of happiness that enjoys a life of its own, independent of their external circumstances.

GOOD CAREER CHOICES

Aquarius Midheaven people are happiest in careers that allow them to work with others in a group environment. They seek a sense of equality in their professional life, to know that everyone is on the same page and working for the same goals.

Unconventional professions appeal to them. They want a career that gives them a chance to be inventive. They definitely need to be in a profession where they can march to the beat of their own drummer. Friendship is part of the picture, and accomplishing group aims inspires them to take charge and achieve success. They will be happiest in a position that gives them plenty of freedom, and support for their innovative ideas and participation in a way that promotes their belief in the equality of humankind.

Self-contentment is assured when they allow the world to see them as a humanitarian – their consistently loving, humorous, friendly self. Success is theirs in any situation which they approach as an original thinker, with a loving understanding of human nature and tolerance for the foibles of others. When they take charge, foregoing the demands of ego and acting for the good of the whole – especially in the service of an ideal – their reward is a feeling of being in control of their own destiny.

PISCES MIDHEAVEN PEOPLE

CREATING SUCCESS

Pisces Midheaven people achieve successful outcomes when they manifest their spiritual or artistic vision. Their ideal profession positions them as a healing, helping influence for others. When they trust that a Higher Power guides their success, they avail themselves of their full share of power.

In their profession, relationships, and finances – indeed, in *every* area of their life in which they accept people and circumstances exactly as they are – they will feel serenity and strength. Their gift of unconditional love helps their situation and gives them a true experience of being in charge of their own destiny.

This may feel scary at first, since they equate their personal survival with keeping the lives of those close to them in good working order. Yet when they release this craving for perfection, when they stop analyzing everything and everyone around them, when they do their part while trusting the outcome to God – their self-imposed burden lightens and lifts.

When Pisces Midheaven accepts others as they find them – without trying to change their behavior – they connect with an abiding love. When they no longer depend for direction upon changing the behavior of others, they are able to feel the bliss of everything around them unfolding in its own proper way.

THEIR ACHILLES HEEL

Pisces Midheaven people are afraid of losing their "safe" role as the logical, practical, down-to-earth voice of reason, and they are often the first to criticize themselves for the slightest wrong turn. This stance is a survival tool they developed in childhood that no longer serves them in adult life. This quest for perfection generally leads to unhappiness, since others are likely to perceive their process as petty, judgmental, and overly concerned with the mundane aspects of life.

Their impulse to overdiscriminate can imprison them in details; nothing they do can measure up to their own standards. The resulting disappointment fosters an overly critical attitude and has a negative effect on social interactions.

Fearing that others will criticize their lack of perfection, their tendency is to keep them at an emotional distance. This "protects" them from those who wish to relate to them on a deep level. In fact, the resulting self-righteous attitude warns *all* who approach that they may box *them* into a category or judge them harshly for some imperfection, perceived or imagined. Their reflexive response is to withdraw; this perpetuates their feelings of isolation, and so the cycle continues.

SELF-ACTUALIZATION

Wherever their vision of perfection shifts its focus from the physical world to the perfection of the universal whole, happiness can enter. If Pisces Midheaven people advance through their life with an attitude of tolerance, having faith that outcomes are as they should be, success will be the byproduct of their journey.

The key is in loving and accepting all things exactly as they are. By keeping their attention on the flawless cosmic order, they will gain a new perspective of *personal* order that transforms daily life. When their vision encompasses the spiritual perfection that underlies all physical manifestation, they will experience consistent joy and well-being.

THEIR "HOME BASE"

Pisces Midheaven's childhood conditioning placed heavy emphasis on organization and planning. They felt a need to be "perfect" – to dutifully fulfill their role so that the family unit could carry on. The value of work was deeply impressed upon them. Their overly structured early years prompted them in adult life to equate security with a carefully organized environment, but this pursuit distracts them from fulfilling their dreams.

Their present survival tools (*i.e.*, keeping their private space organized, overanalyzing everything) lend an illusion of safety, but deeper down an "I'm not perfect enough to succeed" feeling persists. Pisces Midheaven's *true* survival tool will be to value their vision above their fears, to go forth despite their doubts to manifest their dream.

Pisces Midheaven people have had past lives spent in positions of service to others. Therefore their work ethic and sense of responsibility to those under their care is strong; they organize their own life to accommodate those around them. Their inner nature is quite practical and devoted to those they care about.

GOOD CAREER CHOICES

Pisces Midheaven people are happiest in careers in which they can manifest an idealistic vision. They are poetic, spiritual, and artistic

— and when these qualities come together in their profession, they will know that they have achieved success. The idea of healing and making problems dissolve is an important aspect to their work.

To instill in others the vision of a greater trust in Higher Powers at work motivates them to do their best. Pisces Midheaven thrives in a profession in which they can express their awareness of unconditional love and understanding of all people. They need a career that supports their sensitivity and their ability to see the subtleties of life. If they can make a difference and help those who are suffering, their job is a true blessing.

Self-contentment is assured when they allow the world to see their compassionate, non-judgmental, all-accepting, gentle, unconditionally loving, tolerant self: a person of faith in their own vision of intangible spiritual order.

CHAPTER 2

RESOURCES FOR PURSUING GOALS:
The House Containing Your 10th House Ruler

Each of the twelve Houses of your astrology chart is ruled by a specific planet. To locate your 10th House ruler, consult the "How To Use This Book" section. The House containing the ruler of your Midheaven (the Midheaven is another name for your 10th House cusp) reveals extra resources that are available to you – especially for pursuing career goals. These include personal attributes and talents, as well as the energetic resources that you can draw on to help you create success. Although this is most often reflected in your profession, it also holds true for reaching personal goals.

1ST HOUSE

1st HOUSE

If the Ruler of the 10th House falls in the 1st House, reaching a level of professional excellence – or manifesting significant personal goals – requires being a self-starter. These people like to be the hands-on boss of their own area so they can act independently and lead the way.

Following their instincts is a big part of how they create success. To be happy in their career, they need to be valued for their ability to take the initiative. Having an attractive personality is also an asset for them in successfully reaching their goals.

Part of their purpose in this lifetime is to develop their personality by discovering different facets of themselves that they can draw on to create success in the outer world. This includes increasing their capacity for boldness and independent action by making and initiating plans to reach their goals, and then seeing them through to completion. They discover that the more self-reliant they become – in terms of taking personal responsibility for achieving their aims – the more successful they will be in their endeavors.

2ND HOUSE

2nd HOUSE

If the Ruler of the 10th House falls in the 2nd House, the best career choice is one in which the person can draw on their perseverance and their own personal values to create success. For example, I had a client with this position who became an MD. She practiced for a while in conventional settings, and then realized that her motive for going into medicine – to spend time with people and help them heal – was not being met in the world of time-limited doctor's appointments. After taking some time off to get in touch with what she really wanted, she opened her own practice in integrative medicine so she could use her skills and training in concert with her values.

Now she could spend as much time as needed with each patient and facilitate thorough healings. She was so successful that her reputation spread, and eventually she expanded into a clinic. Today she is not only doing work that is congruent with what is truly important to her, but she is also making more money than most MDs. In this same way, these people's own deepest values need to be reflected in their profession – or in what they do to reach their own personal goals – in order for them to blossom and reach their full potential.

Their purpose in this lifetime has to do with discovering their basic value system and what is really important to them. What do *they* feel is worth using their talents and energy to promote and establish in material form? What stimulates and inspires them to develop the self-sufficiency needed to get from point A to point B?

What goals is the person setting to guide their life? By consciously tapping into their ability to persevere, and to proceed one step at a time to create lasting results, they can advance the goals that reflect their deepest values.

Their purpose is also linked to their capacity to make money independently. They have a natural understanding of money, which is one of the assets they bring to their career. For them, money is a barometer of whether or not they are developing the qualities of character they are scheduled to activate and claim in this lifetime. In the process of gaining greater control over their financial situation, they grow in their skills and maturity. Dealing with money in a way that gives them a feeling of self-respect is a path of learning that can bring them great happiness.

3ᴿᴰ HOUSE

3rd HOUSE

If the Ruler of the 10th House falls in the 3rd House, happiness and success will result from choosing a career where they can utilize their gifts for communication, writing, teaching, sales, information-gathering, and logical planning. This person draws on these "people skills" for gaining an understanding of how others think and how words affect them. This can be a huge asset in any business that involves being able to reach people through words and mentally connect with them to exchange ideas. It is through these tools and abilities that they can advance their career, and reach those personal goals that are important to them.

Their purpose has to do with gaining new ideas and ways of viewing life that can further develop and align their way of thinking. They are realizing the empowerment of logic. As they accept the opportunities for learning that life brings across their path – whether through reading books, taking classes, or gaining information from others – they will be exposed to many different worldviews that can lead to a more conscious awareness of their own thoughts. This facilitates their making shifts in their thinking that can help them gain more success and greater peace of mind.

Another part of their purpose may have to do with working out some kind of "karma" from a past life with a sibling or neighbor. They will know if this is true for them by the level of unexplained emotional entanglement between the two of them. Resolving this karma requires them to listen to the other person's position – and accept it as true for *them* – and to be interested in understanding the other's point of view even if it is different from theirs. A willingness on their part to participate in this process can dissolve debate and release the feelings of entanglement. Consciously allowing others to think in whatever way pleases them can lead to feelings of healthy autonomy and self-respect for both parties.

4TH HOUSE

4th HOUSE

If the Ruler of the 10th House falls in the 4th House, having a profession that brings happiness and fulfillment means bringing the element of family closeness into what they do, possibly even working in the family business. They draw upon the power of their natural empathy and ability to understand others' emotions to create success in their career, or in attaining those personal goals that are important to them.

The best profession for them involves giving a sense of security – or some other form of nourishment – to others, perhaps involving the home or food. Examples include real estate, decorating, or restaurants. Nurturing others could also involve creating atmospheres that are reassuring, either mentally or emotionally. Through their abilities to emotionally connect with others to create mutual caring, they advance both their personal and professional goals.

Their purpose in this lifetime is linked to further developing their "internal self" – the basic frame of reference from which they approach life. This may require consciously working to overcome early environmental conditioning, or going through a spiritual or psychological process to reweave unconscious thought patterns that are in the way of their experiencing happiness in life. By releasing those conditioned thoughts and responses that result in feeling emotionally out of control and insecure, they can create a whole new foundation of *positive* thoughts and the feeling of emotional safety that they long for. At the end of the day, it's only the internal work – the growth of character – that they can actually take with them! Then, in the next incarnation, their Soul will begin with a healthier and more positive frame of reference to guide its journey.

Another part of their purpose has to do with family relationships. Since their parents, siblings, and other close members of their family-of-origin are likely to be Souls with whom they have spent time in past lives, it is natural that karma – both good and ill – has accumulated between them. In this life they have the opportunity to work things out with these Souls in a more mutually beneficial way.

5TH HOUSE

5th HOUSE

If the Ruler of the 10th House falls in the 5th House, this person needs to be able to add the elements of creativity and fun to whatever they are involved in – especially in their profession. By drawing on their ability to "bring the mood up" for others and make them feel good, their gift of spreading happiness can be a key to creating success in their career and/or pursuing personal goals that are important to them.

As long as their work is linked to having fun, they can know they are on track. However, if the excitement and fun begin to subside, it is probably time for them to make a change – either in their career or in their approach to their career – in order to continue feeling happy and fulfilled.

Sometimes their career can involve a child. It may even be that raising that child properly, with support and love, can have a lot to do with their purpose in this lifetime. Perhaps this is a debt they owe this Soul from a past life, or it could be that this child's future profession or career will reflect the flowering of their own best potential.

Their purpose is linked to their creativity and following their heart, wherever that may take them. As they pursue activities that bring them pleasure for their own sake, they gain an increased sense of competency and self-respect, and a greater awareness of having authority over their life.

They meet up with their destiny in the process of walking the path that evokes their passion and positive high energy. It may even be that in pursuing their career – or those personal goals that are important to them – they bring something into being through their own creative spirit that has a positive effect in the world at large.

6TH HOUSE

6th HOUSE

If the Ruler of the 10th House falls in the 6th House, reaching a level of professional excellence requires drawing on the ability to work hard and pay attention to details. These people have the gift of a unique sense of synthesis – taking in information, organizing it, and figuring out the puzzle of how everything fits together. This talent is a huge advantage, especially in terms of creating strategies, and their ability for accurate, practical planning is one of their biggest career assets. Another gift is their talent with healing, and a profession that allows them to utilize this attribute would be quite favorable for them.

Their purpose in this life has to do with developing the organizational tools that can help them integrate the various parts of their life, allowing them to create a higher level of order and clarity than they experienced as a child. This includes learning how routines can empower them and give their life a structure that enables them to handle the various details without the wasted effort of repetitive thinking and planning. Cleanliness and organization in the home and office – clearing their environment and their mind of clutter – increases their feelings of competency and leads to a solid sense of self-respect. When they handle the mundane details of life so that their "plate is clear," they feel a sense of being in charge of their world.

Their purpose is also involved with paying attention to developing habits that support them in their daily experience of life. Creating healthy routines in terms of eating, exercising, and participating in recreational activities or enjoyable hobbies are all factors in maintaining a healthy lifestyle. As they take charge in this area of their life, they will find that they gain others' respect and enhance their own sense of self-respect.

7TH HOUSE

7th HOUSE

If the Ruler of the 10th House falls in the 7th House, achieving professional excellence – or excellence in other areas that are important to them – involves drawing on their keen awareness of other people and their ability to recognize and support their identity. Their skills in diplomacy and negotiation are assets that benefit their professional aims. These gifts also extend to the public at large, making them effective and inspirational public speakers.

They are learning how to take charge in their relationships in ways that lead to greater feelings of personal competence, and developing their skills as a good team player. As they learn how to draw on their talent to develop teamwork, their ability to create success blossoms. Marriage can be an important factor in their career, since having a partnership they can count on increases their ability to successfully manifest both their personal and professional goals.

In fact, their purpose during this lifetime has to do with partnership – whether in terms of a spouse, a business partner, or partnering with the public at large. It's possible that part of their destiny involves a partner they have attracted with whom they may have a past-life contract. This would most likely involve a scenario in which they have agreed to support them in reaching their goals, or they have agreed to partner with them so that they can attain their goals. In the process of working out past-life karma with them, they will be empowered to reach a greater degree of worldly success than they ever could have achieved without the influence of partnership.

8TH HOUSE

8th HOUSE

If the Ruler of the 10th House falls in the 8th House, a large part of creating professional success has to do with the gift of tapping into others' psychological mindset, and initiating a change in their emotional state. Their innate ability to discern and understand the other person's values, needs, and motives empowers them to act as a catalyst in shifting their mood into an alignment with more positive energy.

Often, reaching their own goals will depend on their willingness to engage in this "empathetic journey" and to take responsibility for creating a resolution that satisfies the other person's wants and needs in the situation – as well as their own. Other gifts that benefit their career include their instincts for investigation and research, and their talent for grant-writing. It may also be that the resources of another – material or emotional support – are a key to their success.

Their purpose this lifetime has to do with learning more about their own personal psychology and the psychology of others. This involves taking the time to understand other people's motives and needs, and to recognize and appreciate the special resources they bring to the situation. They are learning to discover what others value about themselves – from their point of view. And as they gain awareness of the other person in this way, they can more readily offer solutions that truly address their needs. Then their input for others becomes more appropriate and appreciated.

Their purpose also has to do with learning how to interact in bonded relationships – either sexual or financial – with greater awareness. Making a commitment to engage with another person in this way is not something they take lightly. However, by drawing on their innate understanding of how to do it in a mutually empowering way, and consciously working to establish close, reciprocal relationships, their ability to achieve their personal and professional goals is enhanced.

9TH HOUSE

9th HOUSE

If the Ruler of the 10th House falls in the 9th House, creating professional excellence - and reaching personal goals that are important to them - requires drawing on their own intuitive understanding of situations as they unfold before them. Linked to this is an approach that is guided by their connection with an "inner knowing" of what the next step needs to be in order to reach the desired outcome.

Other assets that they bring to their career include a talent for distributing information effectively to a wider audience, adding the quality of inspiration to whatever they're involved in, and their ability to spread an optimistic attitude to others. Consciously drawing on these gifts, together with exercising their capacity to trust in positive outcomes, is an essential part of their ability to achieve success.

Their purpose in this lifetime has to do with bringing their own personal, spiritual and philosophical perspective into their profession. Because of their innate connection with integrity, ethics, and truth, when they follow the path of right action, their ethical standards shine forth and are demonstrated through their ability to create successful outcomes. As a result, they could be drawn to a profession involving the ministry, or a position in an institution of higher learning.

Since they are also drawn to – and appreciate – all media and artifacts that reflect or express cultural differences, other appropriate career possibilities might include some type of involvement with a museum, or any field involving an expanded awareness of foreign countries.

10TH HOUSE

10th HOUSE

If the Ruler of the 10th House falls in the 10th House, the best career choices allow for demonstrating a willingness to take charge and be the "CEO" of their particular area of expertise. They bring incredible powers of organization to their profession, and have an innate ability to manage others successfully and delegate responsibilities appropriately so that others feel good about helping them reach their goals. Their power to succeed is directly linked to their willingness to draw on their organizational abilities and take on the responsibility of being the person in charge of reaching a goal that helps them rise above everyday concerns.

Their purpose in this lifetime is linked to learning how to take charge in a way that demonstrates responsibility and integrity. This includes learning how to organize others to effectively work together to reach a common goal. They are learning how to lead a more public lifetime and be an example to others by personally demonstrating the principles they believe in. This includes organizing their own life from a practical – rather than an emotional – foundation.

Another part of their purpose has to do with learning how to relate with authority figures in a way that leads to increasing their own sense of self-respect. They are becoming more aware of how to express their own authority in ways that don't diminish others. It is through the process of working with others to achieve mutual goals that they will be able to further develop and refine these parts of their character.

11TH HOUSE

11th HOUSE

If the Ruler of the 10th House falls in the 11th House, achieving professional success – or reaching personal goals that are important to them – requires drawing on the ability to network effectively in group situations. They have an innate talent for taking center stage in a group and leading everyone in the direction of working toward a goal that they know is important.

These talents are powerful assets that they bring to any career. Another asset is that they have the ability to see upcoming trends, and know how to tailor their business dealings to easily adapt rather than being stuck in the past. A knack for relating to others in the context of friendship is also a skill they can draw on to further their goals. Friends are a resource that can help them attain their goals.

They have an innate ability to see the "big picture" and convey it successfully, and this is part of why it is easy for others to come into alignment with them. In fact, their purpose in this lifetime has to do with bringing an awareness of the "big picture" – what it is that can work for everyone involved – into the environment of their career. This includes their natural attunement to equality and their humanitarian attitude.

Some of the friends they connect with during this life may be Souls with whom they share heavy karmic energy from past incarnations. If so, they will experience these relationships as intense connections and they will be challenged to work things out with the friend so that peace can be established between them. This presents a delicate balance for them, since their empathy toward the plight of others can lead them to take on *their* responsibility for success and survival.

However, when they take on responsibilities that are not truly theirs, they are actually robbing the other person of the very growth of character they need to gain by learning to take charge of their own lives. Instead, they are learning to expand their humanitarian instincts to help awaken others to their competence to create success in their own lives.

12TH HOUSE

12th HOUSE

If the Ruler of the 10th House falls in the 12th House, achieving professional excellence requires drawing on their connection with a Higher Power. They have an innate psychic awareness of the intangible aspects of a situation, which also allows them to "see" the best way to resolve it. Their chosen career or profession most likely has to do with manifesting a vision or a private dream. By using their ability to connect with the subtle, unseen forces of life to access spiritual help and insight, they can progress toward reaching both their personal and professional goals.

All of these special gifts give them the ability to reach a wide public audience while staying out of the limelight and remaining a private person. They are extremely sensitive to the subtle forces operating in a situation – the "vibe" between two people, the emotional feeling in a room, the nuances that others are not aware of. They can end up responding to this hypersensitivity by withdrawing from the world, or they can use the same trait to tune in to a personal connection with a Higher Power for guidance and safety. Then they can more confidently reconnect with the environment with their own "spiritual insulation" to support them.

Part of their purpose in this lifetime involves becoming a role model for others by demonstrating their spiritual energy. However, this requires them to go within and ferret out the deep, subconscious, self-sabotaging habits and inhibitions that often block them from success. Then it will be possible for them to contribute to society using their full power.

These old negative patterns have prevented them from experiencing a sense of self-mastery in certain areas of their life where – up to this point – these patterns totally controlled their behavior. To uproot them will mean undergoing a process of self-reflection. This may include the necessity of freeing themselves from addictions – whether to substances, self-destructive behaviors or negative habits. If they are willing to walk this spiritual path, the result will be feeling as though they have emerged from "being in jail" to a state of freedom from deep-seated inhibitions that have kept them from fully expressing themselves, especially in their daily interactions with others.

Their success in the world can be magical. It depends upon their willingness to tap into their Higher Power for help, guidance, and support.

CHAPTER 3

SPECIAL TALENTS:
Planets Located in the 10th House

The planets located in the 10th House indicate the special talents and attributes that the native is destined to manifest in the material world during this lifetime, most often in the public sector through their career. Generally speaking, the more planets that fall in your 10th House, the more important your vocation is to you.

THE SUN IN THE 10TH HOUSE

The SUN brings the following special traits and talents to the native's profession and ability to achieve goals: vital energy, leadership, seeing creative solutions, and a vibrant spirit.

The career is very important to these natives – it's the area of their life that revitalizes them and gives them a sense of purpose. To feel vital and alive, they need to be working with the public in some capacity. Being out in the world, involved with the public and with others in their profession, inspires them to express their talents and creativity and makes their vitality soar!

It is usually better for them to go off to work each day rather than working out of their home. The environment of a public place renews their vitality and helps them to focus their energy. This also applies to other areas of their life. For example, joining a gym is usually a better bet for them than trying to exercise at home.

If the native is a homemaker, they will still need some type of involvement in the public arena in order to fully utilize their leadership skills, stimulate their creative energy, and "recharge their battery." Possibilities might include accepting a position on the board of an organization that they support, or volunteering with a group that directly benefits their family or community.

For people with the Sun in the 10th House, it's always important to have an explicit aim to work toward, since this stimulates their creative energy and inspires them to step into a position of leadership and take action! Having a clear, tangible goal fuels their ability to succeed in any area of their life – personal or professional.

For instance, if their relationship with their mate has become less satisfying, setting a specific goal to enhance it empowers them to take charge of the situation. The goal could be to devise a plan of action for creating more intimacy, having more fun together, improving communication, etc. Or if they want to lose or gain weight, their strongest position for achieving success is to set a "weight goal" and devise a sensible plan for reaching it – including a deadline.

In this lifetime, their Soul has contracted for further growth through refining and integrating their innate leadership ability. Since this is mostly a matter of character development, it requires a willingness to grow in terms of their intentions, motivation, integrity, and maturity. This includes finding out what the others involved in any situation want to accomplish and setting a goal that creates a win-win outcome for everyone – not yielding to the temptation to misuse their creative abilities to reach only their own personal goals.

In every area of their life – career, relationships, and family – the native is learning how to more effectively engage others through expressing their innate gifts. It is a lifetime process of learning how to express their creative leadership abilities in ways that lead to greater self-respect, the respect of others, and achieving leadership positions.

If others are resisting the native's leadership in any area of their life, it is likely that they have yielded to temptation and pursued their own personal goals at the expense of others. When this happens, their best bet is to ask others their goal – what *they* would like to happen in the situation. Then they can reconsider how to readjust the goal – or the manner in which they are taking charge – to better meet the needs of all concerned.

As the native learns – often through trial and error – how to successfully manifest their innate leadership skills, they will achieve greater success in taking charge. And as they gain more public influence, their growth in this area can be measured by the degree to which others recognize and appreciate them and happily follow their leadership.

THE MOON IN THE 10TH HOUSE

The MOON brings the following special traits and talents to the native's profession and ability to achieve goals: empathy, a nurturing spirit, ease in connecting with others, and a caring attitude.

To feel emotionally fulfilled, the native needs some form of interaction in the public arena. Being in the public eye, especially in their career, gives them a deep sense of fulfillment – a necessary component for experiencing true satisfaction in life. They are quite comfortable occupying center stage, and public speaking is very gratifying for them.

When they use their empathetic leadership talents to "take charge" of a situation and unite those involved to reach a common goal, they feel content. By outwardly expressing themselves in the world, they gain a greater sense of inner security. Not only does this bring feelings of completion and of living a well-rounded life, it also engages their ability to nurture others and expands their capacity to create and experience intimacy.

If the native is a homemaker, they will still need some type of involvement in the public sector in order to feel emotionally satisfied. They might consider participating in an organization that works toward goals they believe in, or volunteering with the PTA or another group that directly benefits their family or community.

In all areas of their life, having a clear, tangible goal engages their desire to create security, and this gives them the ability to succeed. For example, if they want to lose or gain weight, setting a specific "weight goal" and establishing a sensible plan for reaching it will activate their "survival drive" in terms of creating a secure and healthy future. This ensures that their "emotional self" is on board, which can give them the energy they need to reach their goal.

In this lifetime, their Soul has contracted for further growth through refining and integrating the expression of their emotional core by utilizing their innate gifts of empathy and nurturing in the public arena. Since this is mostly a matter of character development, it requires a willingness to grow to greater maturity and self-empowerment within this part of themselves.

People who have the Moon in the 10th House have the opportunity for a lifelong growth of character, especially in terms of emotional integrity. The result can include increasing their comfort and security when sharing their true feelings with others. As part of this process, they may even go through many changes in their career – or in the development of their personal goals. They are unconsciously seeking a variety of different experiences to expand their base of personal and emotional knowledge, and their worldview.

In this lifetime, this native is learning how to more effectively express their feelings and their empathetic nature with a greater level of integrity in every area of their life: career, relationships, and family. This includes recognizing that they first need to find out how the others involved in the situation feel about their goal, and take their wants and needs into account as well as their own. This will create more positive results than ignoring or overriding another's feelings to reach their own objective – which the other person may not share.

The challenge is to learn how to express their true feelings more effectively so that others respond in accordance with their intentions. This means being willing to be vulnerable, speaking with others in a way that includes *their* feelings. This is the only way the native's caring nature can find true expression in the world. When they are sharing their emotions with integrity, others are better able to understand and empathize with how they feel, and the native is more likely to experience that sense of belonging that often seems to elude them. This also leads to gaining other people's respect and being put in leadership positions.

If others are currently resisting them in some area of their life, it is probably because the native has yielded to temptation and misused their emotional influence in some way. Should this occur, their best bet is to pull back and consider how they can share their feelings in a way the other person can accept and appreciate, while also taking their feelings into account. It may be that taking the risk to be vulnerabl – revealing *their* concerns in the situation first and then listening to how the other person feels – will open them both to a greater degree of intimacy.

As the native learns – often through trial and error – how to use their emotional influence with integrity, they will create more positive results and take charge in a caring way. The successful expression of their emotional body can be measured by the degree to which others recognize and appreciate their nurturing spirit and happily follow their leadership.

MERCURY IN THE 10TH HOUSE

MERCURY *brings special traits and talents to the native's profession and ability to achieve goals: writing, public speaking, excellent communication skills, logic skills, salesmanship, learning, and teaching.*

To avoid boredom and feel mentally stimulated, the native needs some kind of involvement on the world stage. The public arena is where their talent in communication can best be expressed and can have the greatest influence. The excitement of being in the public eye inspires them to interact with others and share their ideas. For them, the antidote to feelings of boredom or social isolation is to go to a public place and begin exchanging information with others.

A connection with the public sector – which they need to stimulate their mental abilities and the excitement of sharing ideas – usually comes through their career or profession. However, they can also attain it by pursing personal goals that are important to them, through a support group, non-profit organization, classroom, etc.

If the native is a homemaker, it is simultaneously important for them to pursue some type of involvement in the public arena. They might consider volunteering with an organization or group that directly benefits their family or community. Making calls or working on the newsletter would be a perfect match for their talents!

Whatever the native's pursuits, setting clearly defined goals in every area of their life activates their logic and focuses their mind, giving them the power to succeed. For example, if they want to lose or gain weight, their strongest position is to set a specific "weight goal" and design a sensible plan for achieving it – including a deadline. Even just thinking about the goal they want to achieve helps them to become clear, focused, and organized.

In this lifetime, their Soul has contracted for further growth through refining and integrating their communication skills, especially using these gifts in leadership situations. Since this is mostly a matter of character development, it requires a willingness to grow in terms of maturity, self-awareness, and integrity. People with Mercury in the 10th House have the opportunity for a lifetime process of learning how to mentally connect with others in ways that allow them to experience more positive interactions.

In every area of life – career, relationships, and family – they are learning how to more effectively communicate their ideas with integrity. If they use words to try to attain their own goals by outsmarting or outtalking the other person, it's only a temporary win. Neglecting to take the ideas of the other people involved into account may win a temporary victory, but in the end they will "lose the war." If they are not *listening* to the other person, their talk can become a one-way flow of "preaching," which doesn't allow room for others' thoughts. In those instances they may have forgotten that communication is a two-way street, where both people *listen* and ask questions in order to better understand each other.

Communicating with integrity includes honestly sharing their perceptions in a situation, and then being genuinely interested in the other person's ideas. It's important to accept the fact that they may have different – or even opposing – opinions, and honor their right to their own point of view instead of arguing with them to prove that they are "correct."

When the native takes the time to actually find out what the other people's goals are in a situation – instead of just assuming that they are the same as theirs – they can come up with a common, *agreed-upon* goal that everyone can commit to. Then their ideas and abilities become welcome and valued assets that lead to gaining others' respect and being put in leadership positions.

If they find that others are reacting negatively to their communication in some area of their life, it is likely because they have misused their verbal and logical abilities to try to attain their own goals exclusively. When this happens, their best bet is to pull back and reconsider *how* they can communicate in a way that will take the other person's wants and needs into account. Then others will be more receptive to their ideas.

As the native learns – often through trial and error – how to convey their ideas appropriately, they will create more positive outcomes when they take charge. For them, successful growth in this area can be measured by the degree to which others recognize and appreciate their communication skills and happily follow their leadership.

VENUS IN THE 10TH HOUSE

VENUS brings special traits and talents to the native's profession and ability to achieve goals: an expanded awareness of beauty and art, diplomacy, social skills, magnetism, a loving spirit, and a happy nature.

To satisfy their urge to feel loved, people who have Venus in the 10th House need some form of direct interaction with the public. They enjoy being out in the world and feel most alive in public environments! Even their attractiveness is enhanced when they are in the public eye. Being involved in their profession or career, setting goals, and speaking before the public all open their heart and get the love flowing for them. If they're feeling lonely, just go where there are lots of people – browse through a museum, attend a meeting with those who share similar passions and activities, or get involved in a management group – and these natives can generate all the social interaction and loving exchanges they need.

If the native is a homemaker, they will still need some type of involvement in the public arena in order to feel happy and to satisfy their need for social interaction. They might participate in an organization or a group that directly benefits their family and/or community, or get involved with a non-profit organization that promotes a cause that they believe in.

Having a goal fans the fire of their loving nature in any area of their life. For example: if they want to lose or gain weight, their strongest position is to consciously include love as part of their motive in setting a "weight goal," and establishing a sensible plan for reaching it. Having this type of clear, tangible goal fuels their power and ability to find creative ways to succeed.

In this lifetime, their Soul has contracted for further growth through refining and integrating the way they use their social skills. Since this is mostly a matter of character development, it requires a willingness to grow in terms of maturity, integrity, and self-empowerment. Particularly, these natives are learning how to have more integrity in the way they use their magnetic attraction and charm – not yielding to the temptation to misuse their beauty and their diplomatic abilities to achieve their goals at another's expense.

The steps leading to more positive outcomes for them in this area include finding out what the other people involved in the situation want to create – by actively soliciting their ideas and intentions – *before* deciding on a goal. Then they can work with them to establish a goal that will satisfy everyone concerned. They will find that by taking the "high road" they will gain others' respect; their social and diplomatic skills will be welcomed and appreciated, and they will be put in leadership positions.

If they find that others are resisting their social leadership in some area of their life, it is most likely because they have misused their beauty and charm to "lead someone on" in order to reach their goal. When this happens, others may react violently against them. Their best bet is to pull back and consider how they can use their social and diplomatic skills with greater integrity so that others' needs can also be taken into consideration in the situation.

As they learn – often through trial and error – how to successfully express their gifts in social interactions, these natives establish satisfying, loving relationships that are based on mutual respect and appreciation. Successful growth can be measured by the degree to which other people recognize their ability to work things out with others, value and appreciate their gifts, and happily follow their leadership.

MARS IN THE 10TH HOUSE

MARS brings the following special traits and talents to the native's profession and ability to achieve goals: bold initiative, public speaking, courage, independence, and the power to motivate others.

Their career energizes and motivates them to take the lead in bringing about results! To ignite their energy and stimulate them into action, people who have Mars in the 10th House need some form of participation in the public arena or a personal goal they are aiming to achieve. Once they have accepted full responsibility for reaching a goal or overseeing a project, they access the necessary energy to complete the task. Being looked up to as the "authority" motivates them to take action!

If the native is a homemaker, they will still need some type of involvement in the public sector in order to remain happy, energetic, and inspired. They might consider volunteering for the PTA or another group that benefits their family and/or their community. Or look for a position on the board of a non-profit organization that works toward goals they believe in. If they find themselves feeling unmotivated or depressed, just going to a public place can trigger their initiative and recharge their battery!

It's important for them to set goals in all areas of their life, since this stimulates their bold spirit, and motivates and inspires them to take action! For example, if their relationship with their mate has become less satisfying, having a specific goal to improve it (create more intimacy, have more fun together, work on communication skills) empowers them to take the lead and develop a plan of action that can lead to success.

Or if they want to lose or gain weight, their best bet is to set a specific "weight goal" and devise a plan of action to reach it – including a deadline. Having a clearly defined goal fuels their initiative and gives them the fire they need to succeed.

In this lifetime, their Soul has contracted for further growth through refining and integrating their innate ability for self-assertion. Learning how to become more effective in this area is mostly a matter of character development, requiring a willingness to grow to in maturity, integrity, and self-empowerment. Their sexuality is another area that will prompt them to make changes in the way they approach others in order to create more positive results.

A lack of integrity in expressing what it is they truly want in a situation – or, conversely, not taking the wants and needs of the people involved into account – is what leads to negative responses from others. Their temptation is to indulge in anger or misuse sex to try and run roughshod over others – or try to rush their process – in order to reach their own personal goals. However, this will result only in experiencing many situations where they are excluded. Others may let the native know they are "off track" by reacting violently against them and deciding that they just don't want to "play with them" anymore.

In every area of their life – career, relationships, and family – they are learning how to express their boldness, initiative, and courage in new ways that can lead to more positive results. This includes recognizing the importance of having more integrity in the way they take the lead with others.

Honestly expressing what they want, taking other people's goals into account, and being responsible for maintaining open communication are all essential components of providing leadership in an appropriate and positive way that others can cooperate with. Putting these essential elements in place in their interactions with others will lead to their gaining respect and being put in leadership positions.

If others are resisting this native in some area of their life, they may have yielded to temptation and misused their bold initiative in some way – most likely involving sex or anger. When this happens, their best bet is to pull back and re-evaluate the way they have been interacting with others in terms of setting and attaining their goals. They need to make sure that the goals of the others involved in the situation are truly the same as their own and make some adjustments in the partnership.

As they learn – often through trial and error – how to more effectively express their gifts for taking the initiative, they will reach greater degrees of success in demonstrating their ability to take charge. For them, successful growth in this area can be measured by the degree to which others recognize them as an "in-charge" person who takes responsibility. Then others will appreciate their innate gifts, and be happy to follow their leadership.

JUPITER IN THE 10TH HOUSE

JUPITER brings the following special traits and talents to the native's profession and ability to achieve goals: inherent good luck, trust in positive outcomes, the power to inspire others, and an expansive, optimistic spirit.

People who have Jupiter in the 10th House naturally attract "good luck" when they are committed to a situation involving the public sector. They are happiest when their career allows them to reflect their spiritual or philosophical belief system, and inspire others through applying these "spiritual principles." This process fills their heart with expansive, positive energy because they are giving affirmative, inspirational energy to others through being involved with the people at large in some way. These natives have the destiny of doing something good in the world.

To experience their urge for expansion and growth, they need some form of involvement with the general public. If the native is a homemaker, they will still need some type of involvement in the public arena in order to maintain their optimistic spirit, buoyant enjoyment of life, and ability to attract good luck. They might consider a position on the board of an organization doing work that they support, or volunteering for a group that benefits their family and/or community directly.

It's important for them to have specific aims in their personal life, as well as in their profession or career. Having a goal stimulates their innate faith and optimism and inspires them to take charge! Then their positive attitude attracts success, as well as fuels their power to create positive results in any area. For example, if the native wants to reenergize their relationship with their mate, having a definite goal (to create more intimacy, have more fun together, or open the lines of communication) ignites their good luck and empowers them to take charge and set out a clear plan of action to create success.

In this lifetime, their Soul has contracted for further growth through refining and integrating how they use their innate gifts in terms of management and leadership. Through this process they have the opportunity to learn how to use their natural leadership skills – in combination with their underlying optimism and trust in positive outcomes – with greater integrity. This is mostly a matter of character development, requiring a willingness to grow to greater maturity within this part of themselves.

In every area of their life – career, relationships, and family – they are learning to recognize that in any situation they need to determine what the other person's aims are and take them into account *before* deciding on the goal. If instead they use their infectious optimism to talk others into following their plan when it is not benefiting the others' goals – just so they can reach their own personal goal – they betray others' trust in them. Then they will not create the positive results they hoped for, and instead it can lead to disappointment, and possibly even public outrage. They are learning that the situations they create need to be a win-win for lasting success to occur.

The idea is to "practice what they preach" and demonstrate their spiritual beliefs in their own life. If they slow down their process long enough to be honest with the others involved about what they want to achieve – and ask them about *their* goals in the situation – they can use their talents to work out a common goal that everyone agrees on and create a win-win for all concerned. The result of this process is that they will gain others' respect, their positive spirit becomes a welcome and valued asset, and they will be put in leadership positions.

If they find that others are resisting them in some area of their life, they may have yielded to temptation and carelessly misused their talents to achieve their personal goal at someone else's expense. When this happens, their best bet is to pull back and consider how they can take the lead in a way that maintains their integrity and takes others into account.

As they learn – often through trial and error – how to use their gifts as an inspirational leader to create win-win results, they will become more successful in manifesting their belief in positive outcomes. Their growth in this area can be measured by the degree to which others recognize them as an "in-charge" person of integrity, appreciate their innate gifts, and happily follow their leadership.

SATURN IN THE 10TH HOUSE

SATURN brings the following special traits and talents to the native's profession and ability to achieve goals: a businesslike approach, strength, discipline, organization, and the willingness to take responsibility for creating success.

These natives have a "sense of mission" about their life. Even as a young child, they felt that there was something they were "supposed to do" to benefit the world, and they felt a sense of duty about manifesting that mission in the public arena. Consciously they may not even know what the task is, but by taking responsibility for being the

"CEO" in their own life – especially in their career and with their personal goals – they are on their way to fulfilling this charge.

To experience a sense of having fulfilled their destiny, they need some form of involvement in the public arena. If the native is a homemaker, they will still need some type of involvement in the public sector in order to maintain their feeling of self-respect and satisfy their sense of purpose. Public action stimulates their leadership skills and their urge to contribute to the public good, and ignites their power to succeed. One idea is to volunteer with a group that directly benefits their family and/or community. They may do projects in the home that have a public impact, or support one of their children's talents in reaching a public forum.

If the native is not in a situation that allows them to participate directly in a public endeavor, they can still make a difference by writing articles for their local newspaper, or offering to be in charge of a project for an organization that works toward goals they believe in. Even in their personal life, by being an example of principles that they value, they can act as a role model for others.

It's important for them to set clear, practical goals in every aspect of their life. Having a definite aim to work toward stimulates their self-discipline, empowers them to take charge, and fuels their ability to succeed in any area! For example, if their relationship with their mate has become less satisfying, creating a specific goal to improve it (create more intimacy, have more fun together, or open the lines of communication) inspires them to take responsibility with a plan of action to create success.

When they have a goal, it engages their discipline, their serious side, and their ability to see things through to completion. The native must be willing to take total responsibility for creating a success, to be the CEO in their own life. They can delegate, but they need to be the person in charge of the outcome. So for instance, if they want to lose or gain weight, their strongest position is to decide on a "weight goal" and set up a sensible plan to achieve it. In fact, the pressure of a specific time deadline fires up their self-discipline even more!

In this lifetime, their Soul has contracted for further growth through refining and integrating their leadership skills. It is a lifelong process of learning how to be the "CEO" and express their authority with greater integrity, thus creating more positive results. This is mostly a matter of character development, requiring a willingness to grow to greater maturity and self-empowerment within this part of themselves.

Their Achilles Heel is the temptation to usurp the authority of another in pursuit of their own aims. However, if they indulge in this misuse of their influence, the results will be surprisingly embarrassing and they will learn the hard way that they can't run roughshod over others.

It is most often the arena of their career or profession that opens their capacity to grow and learn how to lead in ways that others will look up to and follow. However, in every aspect of their life – career, relationships, and family – they are learning how to more effectively express their willingness and ability to take charge, while maintaining integrity.

For them, gaining mastery in this area means slowing down their process, taking the goals and gifts of the other people involved into account, and showing consideration and respect for them. Becoming a successful CEO requires bringing together the expertise of all the players on their team, and includes recognizing and validating those who help them achieve their aims. And they will find that using their talents in this way not only creates more positive results, but also leads to gaining others' respect and being put in leadership positions.

If they find that others are resisting their leadership in some area of their life, they may have yielded to temptation and become so focused on their own self-importance that they are discounting the others involved and failing to respect their authority. This alienates those who would otherwise be willing to help them.

When this happens, it is a signal for them to pull back and objectively evaluate how they are expressing their authority. They could try asking the others involved how to adjust the goal in ways that would make it a win-win situation for all concerned. When they help to establish a common, agreed-upon goal that all can commit to, they will find that their willingness to take responsibility and see things through becomes a welcome and valued asset.

As they learn – often through trial and error – how to successfully express their authority with integrity, they will be able to create more positive results when demonstrating their executive talents. For them, successful growth can be measured by the degree to which others recognize, respect, and appreciate them as the authority in their area and happily cooperate with their leadership.

URANUS IN THE 10TH HOUSE

URANUS brings the following special traits and talents to their profession and ability to achieve goals: thinking outside the box, taking unconventional approaches, and inventing creative solutions.

People who have Uranus in the 10th House hold innovative ideas about how to create success in business, generally putting them on the "cutting edge" in terms of the decisions they make. They like to be their own boss: having to work through bureaucracy before they can put their inventive plans into action is just too frustrating for them, and strong authority figures bring out their rebellious nature. With their quick mind, they don't have the patience to go along with conventional thinking just because it represents tradition or the "status quo."

With their innate ability to see trends in advance, they are often first to reach a goal that others will later be scrambling to achieve. Their profession or career is usually a special source of excitement for them! Being in the public eye stimulates their capacity for innovation and also activates their need to experience joie de vivre and have the freedom to live life in their own way.

To experience the vitality of new awakenings and awareness, they need some form of involvement in the public arena. If the native is a homemaker, they will definitely need some type of involvement outside the home. Spending time in the public sector sparks their inventiveness, stimulates their leadership skills, and recharges their liveliness. One idea is to participate in a group with similar ideals. Another possibility is link with a group that directly benefits their family and/or community, or accepting a position on the board of an organization that works toward goals that they value.

It's important for them to set goals in all aspects of their life, since having a clear aim to work toward stimulates their unique abilities to successfully manifest their dreams – their way. For example, if their relationship with their mate has become less satisfying, create a specific goal to rekindle the spark (by creating more intimacy, having more fun together, opening the lines of communication, etc.).

Or if they want to lose or gain weight, they can set a "weight goal" and determine a sensible plan to reach it – including a deadline. They may be following their own plan, but they need the structure of a concrete aim to succeed. Having a well-defined goal fuels their innovative thinking, fans the fire of their inventive spirit, and empowers them to take charge and create success in any area.

In this lifetime their Soul has contracted for further growth through refining and integrating their abilities to be unconventional and think outside the box, especially in terms of how they assert their authority. It is a lifetime process of learning how to express their brilliant futuristic thinking in ways that actually lead to successfully accomplishing their goals. Since this is mostly a matter of character development, it requires a willingness to grow to greater maturity and self-empowerment within this part of themselves.

In every area of their life – career, relationships, and family – they are learning how to more effectively express their independent, unconventional nature while reaching their goals in ways that maintain integrity. This includes not using the "shock value" of their unconventional perceptions to try to reach their goal, as this causes others to either react violently against them or to pull away.

Part of this process is realizing that creating a more successful outcome involves taking the wants and needs of the other people involved into account to develop a *mutual* goal, and addressing the possible reactions and concerns of others *before* pursuing a radical approach to attain success. This approach leads to gaining others' respect and being put in leadership positions.

If others are resisting them in some area of their life, it is most likely because they have yielded to temptation and taken a short cut to reach their own personal goal without considering the other person or people involved. When this occurs, their best bet is to pull back and re-evaluate how they can take the lead in a way that truly meets others' needs so that they will be more willing to cooperate.

As they are learning – often through trial and error – how to successfully express their radical energy and unconventional ideas, they will create more positive results in demonstrating their ability to take charge. Their successful growth in this area can be measured by the degree to which others recognize and appreciate their visionary gifts and happily cooperate with their leadership.

NEPTUNE IN THE 10TH HOUSE

NEPTUNE brings the following special traits and talents to the native's profession and ability to achieve goals: visionary insights, imagination, sensitivity, an attunement to psychic realms, idealism, and an artistic, spiritual nature.

People with Neptune in the 10th House have a desire to be part of the flow of Universal Energies – to be emotionally in touch with everything in such a way that they experience it with love. Their profession is especially stimulating to this aspect of their nature. Being in the public eye enhances their capacity to open their heart with compassion and experience the bliss of unconditional love.

To most intensely experience their connection with a Higher Power, they need some form of involvement with the public sector. If the native is a homemaker, they will still need some type of involvement in the public arena to spark their imagination, fuel their artistic nature, and recharge their visionary abilities. One idea is to volunteer at their place of worship, or with some other group that directly benefits their family and/or community. Or they could serve on the board of an organization that works toward goals that inspire their heart.

It's important for them to set goals in every area of their life, since having a clear aim to work toward stimulates their imagination, enhances their ability to visualize a creative plan of action, and empowers them to take charge! For example, if their relationship with their mate has become less satisfying, they can define a specific goal to improve it (create more intimacy, have more fun together, open the lines of communication, etc.). Once they have a clear goal, they'll have a vision for how to bring about the result they desire.

Or if the native wants to lose or gain weight, they can set a "weight goal" and design a sensible plan to reach it – including a deadline. Then they can use their ability to surrender to a Higher Power to take them through the process. Having a clearly defined goal fuels their mystical abilities and generates the energy they need to succeed in any area. However, there's part of them that resists having goals that are too materialistic. There has to be a touch of idealism involved for them to be interested.

In this lifetime, their Soul has contracted for further growth through refining and integrating their creative imagination and visionary spiritual understanding, especially when they use these gifts to take charge. This is largely a matter of character development, requiring a willingness on their part to grow to a greater level of maturity, integrity, and self-empowerment. Through this process they will become more aware of the importance of integrity. This understanding will help them avoid using their capacity for fantasy to delude others, and to stay true to the responsibility of not violating another's trust.

Until a strong sense of integrity is fully integrated into their personality, they may find themselves being tempted to use their abilities to paint a fanciful picture of possible outcomes – that is not necessarily based upon the truth – in order to get others on board to support their own personal goals. They may, at times, even delude themselves when trying to achieve their goals by assuming the role of either the "savior" or the "victim" in the situation.

However, the power of casting an illusion will take them only so far. In the end, if the situation isn't based on reaching a shared goal that truly meets the needs of everyone involved, they will experience a negative reaction. When their capacity for fantasy is too far out of alignment with practical reality, they lose credibility in the eyes of others. They may also lose their trust and experience their anger - and deep disappointment - for them.

In every area of their life – career, relationships, and family – these natives are learning how to maintain integrity when expressing their imagination, idealistic nature, and other visionary gifts. This includes recognizing that they first need to determine the goals of the other people involved in the situation, before thinking they know what the goal should be. Then they can utilize their sensitivity and spiritual grasp of the circumstances to help create a common goal that they are all willing to commit to. Through success with this process, they can gain others' respect and find themselves being put in leadership positions where their attunement to subtle, psychic realms becomes a welcome and valued asset.

If instead they find that others are resisting them in some area of their life, they have probably yielded to temptation and cast a spell of illusion that is not based on the truth in order to reach a personal goal. When this happens, their best bet is to pull back and re-evaluate the situation. How can they adjust the goal – and/or the manner in which they are taking charge – in order to better meet the needs of all concerned?

As the native learns – often through trial and error – how to appropriately express their visionary gifts based on truth and integrity, they will achieve more positive results in taking charge. Their growth in this area can be measured by the degree to which others recognize and appreciate their visionary gifts and subtle attunement to spiritual realms, and happily follow their leadership.

PLUTO IN THE 10TH HOUSE

PLUTO brings the following special traits and talents to the native's profession and ability to achieve goals: the talent of empowering others, charisma, and the ability to act as an agent of change, transformation, and alchemy.

It is by being actively involved in the public arena that this native goes through the transformation that leads to greater self-mastery and personal empowerment. The public sector is where they are called on to take risks that cause them to confront their own inner terrors of exposing their power.

The native may have a tendency to "hold back" from expressing the full extent of their power and potency in the world for fear of reprisal. But if they hide their own Light, they rob themselves of the opportunity to learn important lessons of integrity that bring permanent increases in character and strength. If they are willing to take the risk, they have the opportunity to learn how to express their power in positive ways through the situations life brings them in the public arena.

Though these challenges may terrify them at first, by staying true to integrity and choosing the path of right action they can create a win-win situation, time after time. By taking the risk to walk through this process, they can experience a total renewal of self, access personal fearlessness in their life, and become more powerful and charismatic in the world arena.

If the native is a homemaker, they will still need involvement in the public arena to fuel their vitality and stay on a path of personal growth and empowerment. One idea is to volunteer a for board position with an organization that promotes goals they believe in. Or serve with the PTA or another group that directly benefits their family and/or their community.

It's important for them to set goals in every area of their life, since having a clear aim to work toward stimulates their potency and empowers them to take charge! For example, if their relationship with their mate has become less satisfying, having a specific goal to improve it (to create more intimacy, have more fun together, or open the lines of communication) gives them the energy and sense of personal power they need to take the lead and determine a clear plan of action to succeed in reaching their goal.

Or if they want to lose or gain weight, their strongest position is to write down a specific "weight goal" and a sensible plan for achieving it – including a deadline. Having clearly defined goals fuels their creativity and power to succeed in any area.

In this lifetime, their Soul has contracted for further growth through refining and integrating how they use their gifts of power and charisma, especially in terms of taking charge. Since this is largely a matter of character development, it requires a willingness to grow to a greater level of maturity, integrity, and self-empowerment within this part of themselves. A lifetime process of learning how express their personal power with positive results allows them to claim their rightful position in society.

In every area of their life – career, relationships, and family – they are learning how to use their charisma and their ability to empower others with more integrity. This includes recognizing that they need to determine what other people's goals are in a situation before thinking they know what the goal is. If they try to force them down a path where their goals are satisfied at the expense of others' goals being violated, people will rally against them. And if they obtain their goals by overpowering others, they invite a violent reaction and public disgrace.

If the native finds that others are resisting their leadership in some area of their life, then their best bet is to pull back and reconsider how they can take the lead in a way they will be more willing to cooperate with. Most importantly, are *others'* goals inherently aligned with their own aims and motives?

As they learn – often through trial and error – how to appropriately express their power and charisma, they will create more positive results by taking charge in a way that increases self-respect and the respect of others. For them, successful growth can be measured by the degree to which others appreciate their transformational gifts, recognize them as the authority in their area of expertise, and happily follow their leadership.

NORTH NODE IN THE 10TH HOUSE

The NORTH NODE brings the following special traits and talents to their profession: the gift of being able to be "the boss" in a way that establishes emotional rapport with those they are leading, the ability to achieve goals, and the power to evoke respect and serve as a role model to others by "walking their talk."

Having a goal – and reaching for it – is this person's key to establishing a sense of self-respect and gaining the respect of others. They have experienced many past incarnations feeling trapped in family situations, confined to duties in the home in order to ensure their survival. During these lifetimes they gained a tremendous capacity for emotional empathy and the ability to recognize and address other people's personal concerns and insecurities. Their talent for leadership stems from this innate understanding of how others feel.

Developing these qualities was a necessary part of their role in these past incarnations. However, too many lifetimes at the center of the family – being taken care of by those who went out into the world to meet the group's material needs – has led to their beginning this life lacking a sense of personal competence and self-respect. So now their task is to experience the joy of achieving personal goals!

This requires them to overcome their tendency to be "swamped" by their emotions and learn how to focus on successfully attaining their goals in the world. Through this process they will regain their sense of self-esteem and earn respect from others for their achievements. Goals are their friends in this lifetime. If there is an area where they are feeling vulnerable and overwhelmed, their best bet is to set a goal that requires them to move beyond the perimeter of their own personal emotions. Management positions – managing others or themselves – bring out their best.

For example, if they are feeling insecure about their financial situation, they could set a specific goal they can work toward that will increase their monthly income. Be practical and sensible. Once they are clear on the amount of monthly income that will give them the feeling of safety they need, their next step is to look at their current circumstances and see where the opportunities exist to realize their goal.

If they are married and financially dependent on their spouse, their best bet is to take charge and keep their mind on their goal when discussing this issue with them. An emotional approach on their part will not work. The only way to bring their partner into alignment with them is to present a practical, sensible goal that they can also commit to. They need to "be the boss" in their own mind.

If they are on their own or determine that they need more money than their spouse can provide to feel secure, what are their other opportunities? Perhaps it's time to get a job, find a better-paying job, or look for a second job that can supplement their income. The key for them is to have a goal, and then be willing to focus on that goal

– putting aside emotional considerations – and do the sensible things they need to do in order to reach it.

For a deeper and more thorough understanding of the North Node in the 10th House, consult North Node in Capricorn, in <u>Astrology for the Soul</u> by Jan Spiller.

SOUTH NODE IN THE 10TH HOUSE

The SOUTH NODE in the 10th House indicates many past incarnations where the native was "the boss" – the person in charge who made sure that common goals for the benefit of the family or clan were reached. Having a profession is not an issue for them, since they have had vast experience in taking responsibility for achieving success in many different scenarios.

Because of this, it is natural for them to take charge and try to be the boss in this lifetime. However, any quality of character that is overdeveloped becomes out of balance with the rest of the personality. For them, the qualities of tender emotion and vulnerability were waived in past lives so they could more easily deal with the demands of having to assume so much responsibility.

As a result, subconscious habits can undermine the needs of their heart and Soul this lifetime. If they approach every situation with a "take-charge" attitude, they may be perceived by others as being "controlling." This can rob them of having the experience of being taken care of and protected by the family unit.

It is not that their family doesn't love them – they do. Their challenge is to release their attachment to what they perceive as "ever-looming goals." The idea is to stop postponing the experience of happiness, and tune into what is being offered them in terms of emotional satisfaction in the present moment.

For a deeper and more thorough understanding of the South Node in the 10th House, consult North Node in Cancer, in <u>Astrology for the Soul</u> by Jan Spiller.

IF TWO OR MORE PLANETS RESIDE IN THE 10TH HOUSE

Planets in the 10th House indicate the special talents and traits that the native is destined to demonstrate in the public sector during this lifetime. (See the section specific to each of the planets they have in this House.) Since these urges are meant to be expressed in the public arena, and their career or profession is the most natural environment for this to happen, their occupation is likely to play a very important role in their life. It follows that the more planets occurring in the 10th House, the more the native feels drawn to focus their energy in this realm.

An important point to remember – especially when dealing with two or more planets in this House – is that these are not the attributes that they are meant to demonstrate only through their public interactions. Tenth House planets also indicate parts of themselves that need to be refined and integrated into their personality at a higher level through developing more personal integrity in expressing these urges.

The more planets a person has in the 10th House, the more important it is for them to stay involved in public activities in order to keep their creative fire alive and feel fulfilled. After retirement, it's still important for them to participate in the public sector in some way to keep their vitality going and enjoy life to the fullest. For instance, the native could help those less fortunate by volunteering with a charitable organization that needs their particular skills, or take an active role on the board of their condominium complex.

Even if they're in a retirement home, they need to actively seek a role that calls on their executive abilities in order to feel happy and satisfied. By taking charge and finding ways to stay involved in the public arena, they can remain vital and alive and use their creative gifts in ways that bring them happiness. In fact, being in an environment with a lot of other people can actually enhance their vitality, health, and general sense of well-being.

IF NO PLANETS RESIDE IN THE 10TH HOUSE

If a person has no planets in their 10th House (the house of public activity and power), it doesn't mean that they are never destined to achieve success. It means simply that success for the sake of gaining public recognition or acclaim is not what motivates them. There are other factors that fuel their drive to create a successful life.

For example, if a person has planets in their 3rd House, they may feel motivated to write books or enter a profession that has to do with communication or sales. In the process of pursuing their own natural passion, public acclaim may in fact come of their efforts. But it wasn't part of their initial motivation. Or if they have planets in the 5th House, pursuing their talent for acting could result in achieving fame without its being what motivated them in the first place.

As the native follows the path of their own unique talents and those ventures that energize them and bring them happiness, their efforts can result in public recognition. But the road to fame for its own sake doesn't energize them or stimulate their natural gifts. In fact, leading a public life is not particularly appealing to them. They're not seeking public prominence or necessarily want to have an effect in the public arena.

Although the desire for public attention and making a difference in the public sector doesn't motivate them, they do want others to recognize and respect what they do. Happily, this will be a natural outcome of wholeheartedly pursuing those attributes revealed by the Sign ruling their 10th House.

CHAPTER 4

ADDITIONAL ASSETS FOR SUCCESS:
Houses Ruled by 10th House Planets

The following areas of life come to full fruition through following the professional path - dealing with the general public. These assets are also activated and at the native's disposal when successfully pursuing a personal goal. To see which Houses are ruled by a person's 10th House Planets, see the *How to Use* section of this book.

1ST HOUSE

When the 10th House planet rules the 1st House, the native's personality is given its greatest showcase when they are in the public arena. Their profession actually glamorizes them in some way, stimulating and inspiring their personality to go into action! They shine when the spotlight is on them!

Following the path of their chosen career energizes them physically. It gives them a chance to express themselves in a forum that supports and brings forth the gifts inherent in their personality. Their purpose in this lifetime has to do with manifesting the gifts of their personality in an impersonal way that puts them in the public eye. Their self-identity — who they are without emotional or creative attachment — is given a full chance to be seen and appreciated.

They can always turn to their career or their goals to activate their full self-expression. If they lose focus while pursuing their goals, it's because they have put their ego and drive for adulation above their integrity and the importance of having their goal actualized.

2ND HOUSE

When the 10th House planet rules the 2nd House, the native's values are destined to be expressed and appreciated in a public arena. When they enter into their profession, they take with them the natural gifts bestowed on them from their value system and build for their future in a way that others can benefit from.

Their desire for material security and their inner feelings of self-worth are offered the greatest opportunity for fulfillment and satisfaction by pursuing the path of building a career. Their understanding of money and their natural ease in working with finances can lead to a career in accounting, bookkeeping, or another area where mathematical abilities combined with fiscal acumen are at a premium.

Their purpose in this lifetime has to do with manifesting their values in an impersonal, public arena. What they inherently consider important in life is activated and given full expression when they are actively pursuing their profession or a personal goal. When they go "off track" to reach their goals, it's because they have put the pursuit of personal wealth above their integrity, sacrificing the larger picture that includes the well-being of everyone. They must use their resources to build a solid foundation.

3ʳᴰ HOUSE

When the 10ᵗʰ House planet rules the 3ʳᵈ House, the native's gifts of communication are activated and given the opportunity for full expression in their profession. When they are in the right career for them, everything they have learned and their ability to communicate their point of view, while respecting the viewpoints of others, come into play in the process of pursuing their career.

Their purpose in this lifetime has to do with manifesting their abilities to share information in an impersonal, public arena. This doesn't mean that they have to be on center stage (although they have gifts for doing this), but in some way communicating to a public audience triggers all their fine mental abilities. When they have a personal goal in mind, their capacity for logic and fact-gathering to reach their goal is activated. When they go "off track" in obtaining their goals, it's because they are using their mental skills in a manipulative way, compromising their integrity and straying from the honest facts of the situation.

4ᵀᴴ HOUSE

When the 10ᵗʰ House planet rules the 4ᵗʰ House, the native's emotional capacity for empathy is activated and given full expression in the public arena. Their career gives them a chance to express their caring nature and the strength they have within themselves. Their understanding of family and basic security needs is the tool they bring into the professional arena that helps them shine. Their awareness of the importance of "home" and their ability to express their feelings are additional assets in furthering their career.

Their purpose in this lifetime involves sharing their personal beliefs in an impersonal, public arena. Their gut instincts are activated and expressed powerfully when they are in a public setting. In a nutshell, their professional choice inspires them to express their core beliefs in a form that benefits others. When they go "off track" in reaching goals, it's because their motive is to ensure their own safety and security (or that of their family) rather than use their capacity for empathy to create a bond of caring in a way that works for everyone over the long haul.

5TH HOUSE

When the 10th House planet rules the 5th House, the native's passion and creativity are destined to be seen and appreciated in the eyes of the public. It is possible that one of their children has the potential for tremendous worldly success, or that a creative project they work on will receive wide public acclaim. Through pursuing their career path, their desires for drama, romance, and creativity come to their fullest realization. In some way, their career needs to showcase their special creative talents.

Their purpose in this lifetime involves unveiling and sharing their creative gifts with the public. A strong will is activated and honored when striving toward their career goal, but it can be overpowering when applied to personal relationships. When they go "off track" to reach their goals, it's because they have compromised their integrity and discounted the life goals of other involved parties in favor of their ego — i.e., in search of popularity, romance, or personal pleasures.

6TH HOUSE

When the 10th House planet rules the 6th House, the native's profession inspires them to follow a healthy routine and a work ethic that gains focus and power in their career. Their talent for organization is part of their profession. They bring a desire to be of service to others and an ability to create order out of chaos into their line of business. Their career stimulates their capacity for planning, working with details, and creating healthy routines.

Their purpose in this lifetime has to do with manifesting their gift for taking a disorganized situation and creating order and clarity in an impersonal, public arena. Their natural understanding of health and healing can also be an asset they bring to their vocation. When they go "off track" in reaching their goals, it's because their desire to look good and achieve *personal* success trumps their integrity and trust in a Higher Power that works for the advantage of everyone involved.

7ᵀᴴ HOUSE

When the 10ᵗʰ House planet rules the 7ᵗʰ House, the native's partnerships (possibly including their marriage) are destined to be part of their career. They bring their abilities to form partnerships, use diplomacy to create cooperative alliances, and their gifts for reaching the public into their profession for fullest expression. By being goal-oriented, their capacities for cooperative sharing are activated and satisfied.

Part of their purpose this lifetime has to do with their one-to-one relationships with others, their capacity to be a team player. It's possible that their marriage is a matter of destiny, and through that relationship they learn how to interact more effectively with others. As they pursue their career, their connection with the general public is activated and vitalized. When they go "off track" in obtaining their goals, it's because they have put the motive of manipulating their partner above their integrity and respect for their individuality and preferences.

8TH HOUSE

When the 10th House planet rules the 8th House, the native is attuned to the needs of others and senses what the public wants and values. When they are involved in building their career, their ability to address the public's needs comes into full expression. They also access their capacity to transform others and themselves in the process.

Their purpose in this lifetime has to do with manifesting their understanding of psychology in an impersonal, public arena. In fact, a field that includes and appreciates their psychological insights or investigative talents is truly energizing for them. When they go "off track" in obtaining their goals, it's because they have put the self-motivated aim of achieving a bonus - either financial or sexual - above their integrity and respect for others' personal values and resources.

9TH HOUSE

When the 10th House planet rules the 9th House, the native's spiritual beliefs are destined to be part of their career. They bring their finely tuned intuitive instincts and their connection with a spiritual resource into their profession. Using these gifts, they magically seem to make the right moves that lead to professional success. They grow spiritually in the process of reaching their professional aims. Their career stimulates their ability to respond to situations by means of the spiritual guidance that they receive.

Their purpose in this lifetime has to do with manifesting their optimistic philosophy or spiritual beliefs in an impersonal, public arena. Their desire to be a role model for others inspires them to practice what they preach. Their profession also activates their talent for publishing and distributing ideas they believe into a wider public arena. When they go "off track" in attaining their goals, it's because they have put the motive of "being right" above their integrity and willingness to take into account other people's thoughts and points of view.

10TH HOUSE

When the 10th House planet rules the 10th House, the native's happiest time in life is often spent in professional service. In their career, they aspire to be in a position of authority, and what they learn by being on the public stage can help them to take charge in other areas of their life as well. They are very goal-oriented and feel that the key to their success is reaching professional aims.

Their purpose in this lifetime involves acknowledgment of their competency and their ability to reach goals in a public arena. Their capacity to keep their eye on the goal and to be the CEO directing others is destined to be demonstrated in this lifetime. It is not only their path to fulfilling their sense of purpose, but also the path to personal growth. Feedback from others helps them learn how to be more effective in their work. When they go "off track" in pursuing their goals, it's because they put the motive of letting one of their personal ideals (protecting their public image or wanting to be respected) take over at the expense of their integrity. They have compromised their uprightness and empathic awareness of other people's feelings.

11TH HOUSE

When the 10th House planet rules the 11th House, the native brings their gift of being able to see future trends into their profession, as well as their networking skills and an ability to understand and relate well in group situations. In their career, their talent for friendly and equitable relations comes to the forefront and becomes the key to advancing their goals and achieving success.

Their purpose in this lifetime has to do with manifesting their knowledge — their view of the future — in an impersonal, public arena. They have access to an objective awareness of the big picture involved, and can use this vision to help them achieve their goals. When they go "off track" in pursuing their goals, it's because they let one of their personal ideals or dreams take over at the expense of the group's agenda. They have disrespected the individuality of the other people involved.

12TH HOUSE

When the 10th House planet rules the 12th House, the native brings their gift of psychic sensitivity to hidden forces into their career as a tool to advance their aims. Their vision and private dream find expression through performing on the public stage. Also, the areas in which they don't have it all together yet come to public attention in the arena of their profession. Hence, it's through their career that they can become aware of (and grow beyond) self-limiting patterns of behavior.

Their purpose in this lifetime has to do with manifesting their vision or private dream in an impersonal, public arena. They have the power to put the public in touch with a vision of beauty, imagination, and art that they see. Part of their purpose is to provide the general public with a glimpse of the uplifting vision that they see. When they go "off track" in obtaining their goals, it's because they have fallen into a self-sabotaging behavior (escapism, denial, looking the other way) instead of embracing healthy behaviors as a means to actualize their goals.

CHAPTER 5
YOUR SATURN SIGN
Qualities That Can Help Further Your Career

Saturn, as the ruler of the Tenth House in the natural zodiac, is associated with your job or career.

Your Saturn Sign (the Sign in which Saturn is located in your natal chart) shows the area where you have the most difficulty expressing yourself in your relationships. The closer a relationship is to your heart, the more difficult it is to express the attributes of your Saturn Sign. For example, if your Saturn is in Gemini, you feel blocked in your ability to communicate and connect verbally with others. In highly emotional relationships – your marriage, with your children, and with those with whom you feel the strongest personal love connection - you have the *most* difficulty in communicating and sharing ideas.

In a professional environment, where a non-emotional approach is required, it is easiest for you to express your Saturn Sign. In the above example, Saturn in Gemini people can learn how to engage in effective, two-way communication most easily in a professional setting. It is through their work experience that they learn the "mechanics" of *how* to communicate effectively. Then they can use that awareness of 'what works' when communicating in their personal relationships.

As you consciously begin to express the qualities of your Saturn Sign in your job or career, you gain more ease and confidence with that part of yourself that was the most repressed. Because it is easier to utilize that part of yourself in the work environment, you learn how to effectively express these previously inhibited qualities in ways that create positive outcomes, and this builds confidence and ease in expressing that part of yourself in other areas of your life.

In the process of applying the qualities of your Saturn Sign in your job or career, you also become more successful at work. As you develop this part of yourself through expressing it, over time you will find that your Saturn Sign attributes contain a gift for creating success beyond your wildest dreams.

SATURN IN ARIES

For your best success, consciously utilize these qualities of your Saturn Sign in the workplace: independence; being a self-starter; being the pioneer; taking the initiative.

SATURN IN TAURUS

For your best success, consciously utilize these qualities of your Saturn Sign in the workplace: building slowly for lasting results; step by step processes; perseverance; loyalty; the enjoyment and appreciation of life as it is.

Additional Assets For Success

SATURN IN GEMINI

For your best success, consciously utilize these qualities of your Saturn Sign in the workplace: communication; reading; learning; teaching; writing. Being interested in other people's ideas, sharing your thoughts, and exchanging information to get at a solution reaps huge rewards.

SATURN IN CANCER

For your best success, consciously utilize these qualities of your Saturn Sign in the workplace: nurturing; being interested in co-workers' personal lives; supporting others to help them feel better; empathy; caring about co-workers.

SATURN IN LEO

For your best success, consciously utilize these qualities of your Saturn Sign in the workplace: enthusiasm; inspiring others; loyalty; creativity; leadership; determination; creating your own destiny.

SATURN IN VIRGO

For your best success, consciously utilize these qualities of your Saturn Sign in the workplace: being of service; awareness of others' physical needs; organization; attention to detail. Helping co-workers in practical ways goes a long way toward creating your success.

SATURN IN LIBRA

For your best success, consciously utilize these qualities of your Saturn Sign in the workplace: teamwork skills; supporting others; peacemaking; diplomacy; cheerleading; creating attractive presentations. Being aware of fairness in relationships with co-workers helps to create your success.

SATURN IN SCORPIO

For your best success, consciously utilize these qualities of your Saturn Sign in the workplace: bonding for mutual empowerment; creating joint partnerships for mutual gain; initiating transformational changes; being aware of the psychology of others—their needs and motives.

SATURN IN SAGITTARIUS

For your best success, consciously utilize these qualities of your Saturn Sign in the workplace: optimism; awareness of 'silver linings'; trusting life; chivalry; helping others because it's the right things to do.

SATURN IN CAPRICORN

For your best success, consciously utilize these qualities of your Saturn Sign in the workplace: management skills; executive mind-set; discipline; talent for achieving goals. Being willing to 'be the boss' and take responsibility for creating positive outcomes goes a long way toward establishing your success.

SATURN IN AQUARIUS

For your best success, consciously utilize these qualities of your Saturn Sign in the workplace: friendliness; objectivity; taking a scientific approach; seeing the 'big picture' and conveying it to others to create a group success.

SATURN IN PISCES

For your best success, consciously utilize these qualities of your Saturn Sign in the workplace: compassion; understanding the plights of others; gentleness; sensitive communication; helping others through healing and soothing.

Conclusion

I hope that the information presented in this book has helped illuminate the ways in which you can use your inborn gifts and talents for achieving worldly aims. Many people ask: "Will I be successful?" The answer is, it's up to you. We always have free will, and it's a matter of how you choose to align with your own internal design.

Another more theoretical question is: For purposes of evolution, did the Soul consciously choose to incarnate in the moment that gives the native certain predictable experiences -- areas of conflict or ease? Does each of us have a greater purpose or intention behind our individual internal wiring as revealed in our astrology chart? If so, then perhaps the difficult aspects in our charts show areas that we didn't handle correctly in a past life (karma). By focusing on these areas with greater awareness and personal depth, we can fully understand and consciously resolve them in this lifetime (dharma).

The troubled Houses in our chart certainly give us a lot of motivation to more deeply understand the areas of life ruled by the Houses involved. Out of this internal conflict comes the benefit of outecreative action that furthers humankind, whether the stage is the people in our immediate circle or in a public arena.

Visit WWW.JANSPILLER.COM

The official website of JAN SPILLER for empowerment on the spiritual path

FREE Services:
Daily Horoscopes
Astrology Phenomena Tips
FREE Birth Charts
Power Wishing Well
Special Power Tips
Astrology 101

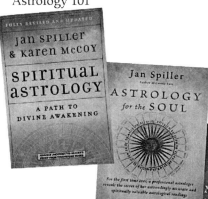

Special Membership Services:

Unlimited GODDESS ORACLES Access
New Moon and Full Moon Reminders
Exact Best Times for New Moon Wishing
Numerology Forecasts

ALSO AVAILABLE
Personal Astrology Reports, Private Consultations and much, much more...

CPSIA information can be obtained at www.ICGtesting.com
Printed in the USA
LVOW08s0535300415

436702LV00001B/110/P